Here Is My Hand

Here Is My Hand

THE STORY OF LIEUTENANT COLONEL ALIDA BOSSHARDT OF THE RED LIGHT AREA, AMSTERDAM

by

DENIS DUNCAN

HODDER AND STOUGHTON
LONDON SYDNEY AUCKLAND TORONTO

Copyright © 1977 by Denis Duncan. First printed 1977. ISBN 0 340 21678 6. All rights reserved. No part of this publication may be reproduced or transmitted in any form or by any means, electronic or mechanical, including photocopy, recording, or any information storage and retrieval system, without permission in writing from the publisher. This book is sold subject to the condition that it shall not, by way of trade or otherwise, be lent, re-sold, hired out or otherwise circulated without the publisher's prior consent in any form of binding or cover other than that in which this is published and without a similar condition including this condition being imposed on the subsequent purchaser. Printed in Great Britain for Hodder and Stoughton Limited, Mill Road, Dunton Green, Sevenoaks, Kent, by C. Nicholls & Company Ltd., The Philips Park Press, Manchester, M11 4AU.

Contents

Acknowledgments

I acknowledge gratefully the willing co-operation I have received in the preparation of this book from Lt-Colonel Bosshardt and her colleagues in the Goodwill Centre in Amsterdam, Commissioner Kathleen Kendrick of The Salvation Army's Headquarters' staff in London, Commissioner Verwaal, Amsterdam, Lt-Colonel Harry Dean, and other officers of the Army. I also express my appreciation to Jillian Tallon who has typed and re-typed the MSS with care and concern.

Prologue

I GLANCED ANXIOUSLY at the clock as I tidied up my desk, the day's work at home done. The diary told me that I must be on my way into Central London by four p.m. I was due to fly to Amsterdam that Friday evening to see Lt-Colonel Alida Bosshardt.

I had been to Holland on several occasions, but never to Amsterdam, so the visit was intriguing for its own sake. But I knew too that this particular visit had much more to it than just the experience and enjoyment of a new and interesting city. I had special work to do in it. And the focal point for that work was Colonel Bosshardt.

I had heard quite a lot about the work of this Dutch Salvation Army officer. I had also heard of her national fame and reputation. I had been told by people who knew her that she was one of Holland's most outstanding and revered figures. She was widely known in her own country for her work and ministry, and several books about that ministry had been written in Dutch. But there was nothing in English as yet. So I had been asked if I would do something more to make her work known and tell in English, for the English-speaking world – and perhaps even beyond that – the extraordinary story of her quarter-of-a-century's work and more in the Red Light area of Amsterdam.

The project appealed to me in many ways, but I had one hesitation. So much of my work in recent years seemed to involve counselling in the sexual area that the prospect of having to write a book in which, inevitably, that area must (or so it seemed at first sight) play a large part, discouraged me. I constantly felt angry that, in contemporary society, this aspect of life was so often separated from its total context of love and commitment as if it were some self-sufficient aspect of life, reducible to techniques and valid as an exercise on its own, out of its true context. Did this mean I would have to investigate the contemporary prostitution, on a large and public scale, of that which should be sacred and spiritually satisfying? Did it mean I must be in close contact with the most blatant and blasé commercialism possible – for was not Amsterdam one of the most 'advanced' cities in the world so far as contemporary pornography and permissive behaviour was concerned?

I hesitated on this ground alone until I realised that, of course, the importance of Colonel Bosshardt lay not in the situation itself but in what she was doing within that situation – and had done for more than twenty-five years. To look into this piece of witness would be uplifting, not degrading.

I had to go and see what this woman was doing, I decided. She alone would convince me one way or another.

The forty-minute train journey from Victoria Station in London to Gatwick Airport passed quickly. There had been, so far, no time to re-orientate my mind to the undertaking I had to face. By the time the train reached Gatwick, I had done little more than sort out papers and tickets. Amsterdam as a reality still seemed far off.

There were but ten minutes before take-off as I hurried down the interminable corridors towards the plane. The last gesture was the now (sad to record) inevitable 'frisking' – a security measure that surely symbolises the insecurity of our modern ways of life. That completed, I was on my way to Amsterdam.

Comfortably settled at last, with forty minutes' flying time ahead, I took out the notes and correspondence I had about Colonel Alida Bosshardt.

I had written to Colonel Bosshardt asking her not to go to any trouble to meet me. As I was uncertain when I could get away, it would be easiest if I simply arrived 'mid-evening on Friday' and made my way into Amsterdam. I knew that Friday evening was a particularly busy one in the Bosshardt programme and that she would be out on her regular rounds, but so long as she left a message at the Goodwill Centre as to where she was, I would find her. As for hospitality, there was no need to worry. I would fix myself up in a hotel in the city for the two nights in order not to complicate her life in any way. I did not therefore inform her of my arrival time. This arrangement would also leave me free to feel my way into a country I as yet knew only slightly, a city which I did not know at all, and a situation I had never encountered.

It seemed no time till we were descending in the evening light towards Schiphol Airport. Though the sun had gone down, it was possible to see the symmetrical landscape below – the square and rectangular fields, the long straight canals and the visible expression of the tidiness and order I always associated with Holland. And of course, there they were, the inevitable motorways, part of contemporary life everywhere, busy as always, bisecting the fields below just as the canals did.

It was not much more than two hours earlier that I had hurried away from home and the work which had occupied me that day. Now I was facing the unknown, open-minded as to what I should find, intrigued to know what the famous Colonel Bosshardt was like in the flesh.

I did not have long to wait. I walked through more long airport corridors – for airport construction the world over seems to be of a pattern – to the baggage reclaim area. My hold-all recovered, I made for the exit, to look for the usual sort of transport to the city that all airports supply.

I saw a cluster of people around the exit, chatting, laughing, hand-shaking. In the centre and certainly the focal point of the group was a lady in the uniform of The Salvation Army.

It could only be Alida Bosshardt.

It took a little time for Colonel Bosshardt to disengage herself from her admiring audience. I introduced myself and expressed surprise that she had come to meet me and, even more, guessed the right plane. She had taken a chance and was glad she had been right.

'But we must hurry,' she said. 'I have to be in the Club by nine o'clock.'

We made for the exit, but even as we did so, a voice cried out 'Colonel Bosshardt, Colonel Bosshardt.' She turned, as excitedly hurrying towards her was a man in his thirties, a member, obviously, of the airport baggage staff. There was a quick and happy handshake, a brief exchange of greetings and we were on our way again. 'He used to be an alcoholic,' she said. 'I helped him. Now he keeps a good job.'

Colonel Bosshardt looked anxiously at her watch again. 'Come quickly,' she said, 'the football men at Ajax will wonder where I am.'

Ajax? She could only mean the famous Dutch football club whose name was known and respected wherever the game was played. It was the club to which

Johan Cruyff belonged before he moved to Spain. It was the club that had given so many of its number to Holland's national team.

'You will come with me?' said Bosshardt. (I have since become used to the, for me, unnatural but, in Dutch Salvation Army circles at least, accepted way of using her surname only. In her case, it carries a feeling of respect and admiration).

'Of course,' I replied. 'You just do whatever you always do on a Friday night and I'll happily come with you.'

A small car stood right outside the airport door. I looked with amazement. Could there be an airport in the world where you park your car just *there* without dire consequences? Perhaps there are, but on treble yellow lines (Dutch style)? The Bosshardt car stood there serenely straddling an area so clearly marked and painted that no one in their senses would have risked the wrath that must inevitably come from such obvious law-breaking.

There was a piece of paper on the windscreen, held safely by the wipers. On it was scribbled in her own writing: 'Bosshardt'.

It was enough. No one in Holland would dream of prosecuting, booking or even moving anything belonging to this obviously loved and respected figure.

It had not taken long to prove in fact what I already knew in theory – that I had come to see an extraordinary woman.

That car on that forbidden territory said it all.

1

On A Friday Night . . .

FRIDAY NIGHT IS a fixed point in the Bosshardt diary. This in itself is significant for that diary is a conglomeration of events – meetings, speaking engagements, services, interviews, visits, broadcasts, etc., etc., – that make every week different. So what any day may bring to pass in the Bosshardt life is anybody's guess. But never on a Friday.

I was soon to find out why this was so.

For many, many years Bosshardt had to do all her work on foot or by bicycle. Now that she has her little car, she knows the difference ease of movement has made to her. Our journey towards Amsterdam, first along typical arterial roads and motorways, then into suburban streets, was quick, bright and occasionally exciting. Colonel Bosshardt would point out this and that, talking enthusiastically all the time and using her hands freely to show me a building, a street, a development that she thought interesting. Despite the inevitable hum of the car's engine, I was able to follow her adequate English reasonably easily. Only the intonation – a typically Dutch intonation – blurred this word or that.

Quite soon we turned off the main street and into the parking area of the Ajax football stadium. She grabbed her satchel full of *War Crys* and we set off up the steps to the supporters' club attached to this celebrated team. It was typical of any social club of its kind – noisy, busy, convivial. Some played snooker. Some sat and talked. Some were watching the replay of a recent international match on television, and these I joined. I was introduced to the club manager who sent a cup of coffee for me to drink while Colonel Bosshardt went on her *War Cry* rounds.

How important, in financial as well as evangelistic terms *War Cry* was to the Goodwill Centre I was to learn later. Meantime I was impressed, as I have been in every situation in which I have seen Bosshardt, by the genuine enthusiasm that appeared at every level whenever she entered a hall, room, hospital or house. This was made possible and perhaps inevitable by her wholly extrovert approach to everyone. Be it workman, alcoholic, princess, prostitute or peer, her attitude was the same, her greeting warm, her comments frank, her friendship real. I did not yet know this popular 'envoy of the Lord', as I had heard her described. I could not be sure where this natural ability to get alongside people came from. I was not, on first acquaintance, certain our wavelengths were the same, but by the time we left the Ajax stadium, I did know I was in the company of someone whose integrity, sincerity and dedication were in doubt to no one in that city. I was not there to analyse personality or motivation, nor to slot a significant personality into some psychological box and label her some 'personality type'. No slick summing-up of the personality make-up of this or any other pioneer does justice to the range, value and effect of the work they do.

I had only had an hour or so with Bosshardt so far, but I saw her going about 'doing good'.

To tell of that kind of goodness is to encourage others to 'go and do likewise'.

I had decided already I would tell the story of this 'envoy of the Lord'.

It was after nine thirty p.m. when we left the Ajax stadium. Again I sensed time was all important as Bosshardt threw her briefcase into the car. Another moment was needed for her to stop at the caretaker's door – and how important consistency in caring was to Bosshardt was already evident – pass in a *War Cry*, say 'hello' to the family, and then we were off again. We had to be in 'my district' by ten if possible.

In the early Middle Ages, Amsterdam was no more than a little fishing village, situated by and around a dam across the Amstel, a tributary of the Rhine. Today Amsterdam is an international city, a centre of culture, commerce, industry and tourism. It is the largest city in the Netherlands with a population of around eight hundred thousand and industrial activity far beyond any other Dutch city. Despite this, it does not have the drab and dreary appearance typical of so many cities. In fact it is ringed by a sequence of garden cities built after the two World Wars. The old city is famous for its canals, its numerous historic buildings and its seventeenth- and eighteenth-century façades.

It was to the heart of that old city, in the Centrum area, that Colonel Bosshardt was driving me that Friday night, for her district was the famous 'Red Light' district of Amsterdam. And it was in that same district she had lived and worked for quarter of a century and more. It had been her life's work. Whatever the Red Light area meant in trade or tourist terms, for Bosshardt it was home.

It was now too dark to see the detail of the inner part of the city as we motored through it. Bosshardt was still pointing to this and that – a museum, the road that led to Anne Frank's house, a park, a canal.

It was towards ten o'clock and the canals seemed to

be more and more frequent. Trams thundered along the streets, their presence and practice familiar to the local population. I thought, with memories of similar situations, of the problem streetcars can pose to the foreign driver already on the wrong side of the road and threatened by fast turning trams from unexpected directions.

We turned off the main, wide street and suddenly seemed to be in streets as crowded and narrow as to make driving impossible. Bosshardt was used to the hazards of her home ground. It seemed natural to go at speed through incredibly small spaces, send pedestrians scuttling to safety to right and left, miss bicycles and other vehicles by inches and somehow arrive at our destination having received and given no injury or scratch.

'This is my district,' said Bosshardt – and it seemed proudly. Home is where you belong and Bosshardt belonged here.

It is hard to know how to react to strange and unfamiliar circumstances. It seemed too soon to try and do so in the Red Light district of Amsterdam that night. It was but four hours or so since I had been at work in the familiar surroundings of London. To be so soon transported to a strange area in a strange city demanded too much. I delayed the forming of judgments. I was in the hands of one who was at home here, and had committed myself to the Friday night sequence. I must let it unfold.

The district Bosshardt looked on as home, which the world calls the Red Light area, is made up of an interweaving of canals and streets. It is between the Oosterdok and Rokin-Damrak main streets that change name at the famous Dam. The Damrak ends at the

Central Station. You enter the area easily from the region of the station – and in doing so arrive quickly at the Goodwill Centre in O. Z. Voorburgwal. It is also easily reached by walking away from the Dam Square down Dam Straat which leads directly to the O. Z. Voorburgwal. In going that way, you pass the Salvation Army headquarters.

The O. Z. Voorburgwal and Achterburgwal are narrow one-way streets, the 'one-way' part depending on which side of the canal you are. The narrowness of the streets is accentuated by the use of the part directly next to the canal as parking space. These and other similar streets make up the Red Light area.

The canals are tree-lined and the streets cobbled. In the morning when all the activities of the area are at a minimum, and the ordinary shops like grocers, butchers, etc., ply a normal trade, it is a pleasing, picturesque arca, full of character and charm. But our arrival time was just after ten on a Friday night, so the streets were crowded with sight-seekers and sight-seers, multitudes of people there to see something that has become an international tourist attraction, some to savour the dubious delights of a world dedicated to sensual satisfaction.

It is a fact of modern life – and perhaps indeed of life in every age – that there is gain to be made on a vast scale from the gratification of the sexual instinct in man. The Red Light area in Amsterdam like Soho in London, and similar areas in most of the world's major cities, exists and grows because enough of the public want it to make it pay. There are however differences both in the way it is done and in official attitudes to the trade in lust. An examination of that question in sociological or any other terms is out of place here. Amsterdam has made its position clear. Prostitution is neither legal nor illegal. It is simply accepted as a fact, tolerated as a necessity, best contained if possible within an area, and useful in commercial terms – as the tourist attraction of the area bears out.

The Dutch are a practical people. It is not easy for the somewhat perplexed visitor from other cultures to work out how and why a country with a rigid and moralistic religious background such as that represented historically by the Dutch Reformed Church can throw up permissive attitudes on a scale as yet unmatched or at least not surpassed in public terms by any other country in the world. That again is a big, but here not wholly relevant question, part of the answer to which is fairly obvious. What is reality is the fact itself and this is probably a tribute to the Dutch flair for providing what is needed *if* it is needed in a big enough way. So equally some years ago the Vondelpark was left to the hippies as a place of free behaviour and gay liberation movements are allowed to proliferate in Amsterdam. The Vondelpark happily now has been restored to its original glory and hippies, etc., are not allowed to camp or sleep there. Alternative facilities for youngsters needing shelter have been made avail able at very cheap rates.

Strangely enough the immediate impact of the Red Light area is not as sordidly unpleasant as might be expected. The whole trade and its implications simply cannot commend themselves in any way to those (of any philosophy) who see sexual intercourse as, ideally, the ultimate expression of a totally loving and committing relationship. That said, the facts are simply there, and as Bosshardt's particular work relates to these facts, I can only try to describe the situation as objectively as possible.

'The Dutch love their whores,' said one highly intellectual Dutch lady when we discussed this issue. I feel this to be true though it is not the purpose of this book to analyse what it means. What I did feel from Bosshardt as we moved into 'her' area was not a sense of shame, but rather a sense of pride; not a pride over what was done there, of course, but pride in relation to the kind of people who lived and worked there. And her references to the quality of people in that area in terms of friendship, relationship and community, always included 'the girls'.

To the attitudes of officialdom, the Church and the community to all that the Red Light area stands for and is, I shall return. Let me stay with that Friday night – for Amsterdam, for Bosshardt, for the Army officers, a typical Friday night. Yes indeed, I stood in a strange and unfamiliar world in so many ways, but there was no time for analysis and questioning and certainly none for passing thoughts about how on earth I had got into such a situation! The car stopped suddenly outside one of the canal-side buildings on the O. Z. Voorburgwal and Bosshardt, grabbing her satchel of *War Crys*, was out. 'Come and see our hostel,' she said.

We climbed the short outside stairway to the Gastenburgh and Bosshardt, striding out and always apparently attacking situations, stepped into a canteen-cum-T.V. lounge-cum-recreation room. Sister Henny, whom I was to meet again, was on duty. She was younger than Colonel Bosshardt and was one of her assistants. As I found out later, she, her husband – a Salvation Army official but not a uniformed officer – and family lived in a flat above Bosshardt at the Goodwill Centre, so she was able to give 'on the spot' help at any time.

Sister Henny was serving at the counter as Bosshardt strode in, shouting greetings to all, laughing with this one or that. Those in the hostel were from the lower rungs of the human ladder. Indeed apart from the sound of Dutch, I felt I could have been in any Salvation Army social work refuge anywhere in the world. This was The Army 'on the job', more expert than any organisation or church that I know at communicating with the 'outs' and 'downs'. 'It is a "dry pub",' laughed Bosshardt.

Another flowing Dutch conversation, and I was aware 'the English preacher' was being announced. (I had repeatedly to remonstrate with Bosshardt over the important differences between 'English' and 'Scottish' and the unforgivable sin of confusing them!) The chorus of grunted greetings in my direction made the exchange clear. One man, a history of suffering and illness crying out from his twisted body, was quick to show his skills in the English language. He was an ex-merchant seaman whose life was now made up of hostel and hospital alternately. It was 'hostel' at the moment, as Bosshardt explained to me on the next section of our journey. She was in constant touch with him in his hospital times too.

Bosshardt disappeared – no doubt to distribute a few more *War Crys* – and it was Sister Henny who was left to show me the women's hostel at 'the Ruytenburgh' and the meeting house there. But of these more later. Meantime, it being a Friday night, we had to hurry to the next part of the Friday programme – something that has been a Friday night feature for over twenty-five years.

It was a fine June night that Friday, my first ever in Amsterdam and in the Red Light area of the city. As I walked along the streets and by the canals, there was much that was pleasant and some that even deserves the description lovely – the buildings of character, the trees, the lights, the barges, the bridges. I do not know the comparative areas of other European cities so I can pass no universal judgment on such areas. I know, in a general way, the Soho area of London and I cannot think of any other word but 'sordid' to describe most of its streets – Soho Square apart, perhaps. But, so far as Soho is concerned, I sympathised with the young man from my former church in Glasgow, who turned up in London with his fiancée on the night he became engaged. To show hospitality and friendship to them, I had taken them by car on an evening tour of the city. Part of the journey took us through the Old Compton Street–Frith Street–Greek Street–Brewer Street–Bateman Street area. 'You can smell the evil,' he said. I did not disagree. The trade in lust seemed to pervade the area with its seamy strip-tease shows staffed by suspicious-looking characters and its 'model' doorbills, one of London's answers to the laws that cleared the streets of the visible prostitute and created call-girl rackets, phoney advertisement methods and sleazy clubs as a cover-up for a still flourishing business.

It did not feel quite like that in Amsterdam that night – to my surprise. Perhaps it was the canals that created space. You could see the sky and the stars through the trees. Perhaps it was the system. With prostitution tolerated, 'the girls' (to take Bosshardt's word) could display their wares freely. So it was the accepted method of business that each girl – or two together – should hire, by the day, small rooms and so seat themselves 'in the shop-window' that all could see and judge for themselves the services offered. There were many coloured lights in the obviously comfortable rooms, often with attractive curtains and decoration, and the streets were brightly lit, while the canals offered back reflections from the water and so made yet another contribution to the multi-coloured gaiety of the area. The sound of music from this club or that added its quota of apparent glamour to this quaint and curious quarter of a city.

That the Red Light area has become a tourist attraction popularised in the travel brochures of the world is obvious. The packed streets, narrow indeed where no canals split them in two, resounded to chatter and comment in many languages. Many twos, threes and parties sauntered through the streets with no intention of involvement of any kind, but simply to see the sights. This particular development in jet-age travel and package holidays, of Americans 'doing' Europe and Japanese overflowing from their claustrophobic country to see the world, is not welcomed by the girls – for obvious reasons. They are there to make money and to seek trade. They have hired their rooms or stance and are paying the price. They want 'work'. To have gangs of gawping tourists use them as a free peep-show is frustrating, irritating, infuriating – and humiliating. For them, this is a prostitution of prostitution.

I could already feel a sympathy developing for the girls – as I had already felt it in Bosshardt and some of her colleagues. But there is another side, and to this one must come to put the picture in perspective. I suspect the older ways of the area to be altering. Perhaps the pleasanter aspects I have spotlighted once were dominant and the 'oldest profession' was carried out in a corner – public, but still only a localised part of a very large city – with some understanding, rules and even courtesies. But today sin is big business and sex is, for those who can commercialise it, a road to prosperity. The truth of this was evident in the other aspects of the district's life – the innumerable sex-shops, bookshops and film shops/studios advertising their wares in sound, colour and light and worst of all, the numerous voyeur presentations, advertised in appalling terms, performances reducing the creative action of human beings to a public peep-show on the grand scale. It seems that the ultimate in permissiveness has been reached, when, night after night, performance after performance, young people drawn from – one wonders where – prostitute for their own and others' gain the most sacred act in human life.

As I walked with Sister Henny towards the Goodwill Centre, I felt as I had feared, some kind of involvement in degradation, and yet here I was with an officer of obvious integrity, maturity and sensitivity who radiated wholeness and holiness, for whom this was not only home for her and her children, but also the backcloth to ministry, a backcloth that remained a backcloth and did not impinge in any way on her or her family. This, at that moment, created for me a contradiction – or at least a paradox. It was hard to understand. Indeed it underlined so many questions in my mind about the Dutch and their apparent contradictions – at least to an 'English preacher' – not least the attitudes I felt in Bosshardt herself about the nature and purpose of her work. I hoped time, familiarity and insight would begin to put things right, or at least in perspective.

But one thing more worried me. I *felt* more than saw violence or potential violence in this situation, for sex and money together create venues for violence, blackmail, protection rackets and so on. I did not know how house-renting, premises, etc., functioned here, but I could feel, intuitively, violence in the air. I felt my colleague didn't. So questions lingered in my mind as we moved towards the Goodwill Centre. Then I heard music – melodeon or accordion it seemed, and voices male and female. I recognised the tune. The words were indecipherable, but I had no doubt what they said. 'What a Friend we have in Jesus,' I said to Henny.

'Yes,' she said. 'Come, we must join them. They've already begun.'

It was Friday night.

Every Friday night for the last twenty-eight years there has been music and melody ringing round the narrow streets of the Red Light area and across the picturesque canal bridges.

Nader, mijn God, bij U.
U naderbij,
Zij ook de weg daartoe
Een kruis voor mij.
Wat dan mijn toekomst zij
U nader, naderbij.
Nader, mijn God, bij U,
U naderbij.

Who would have believed it? Six hours earlier at four o'clock I had been quietly doing part of my normal work in the peace of my London home. Now at ten thirty p.m., I found myself singing 'Nearer, my God, to Thee' on a canal bridge in Amsterdam's Red Light area in Dutch with members of The Salvation Army. It was hard to know if this was reality or part of a dream created by the invitation to write this book. I looked at the group to which I now belonged. There was the older man who played the melodeon. There was Henny and a number of other officers in her age group. There was a much older officer who, as we moved from singing point to singing point would hive off into this or that set of rooms, where, because of the open curtains, she could be seen talking to some of the girls. There was a young man, an actuarial student as I later found out, who was giving assistance to the Goodwill group not only by his involvement in the Friday walk but through his analysis of the finances of the Centre and some costing of its future work.

The procedure was simple and familiar to those who know these Friday nights. The Army would march from one selected point to another, led by the Army flag, held proudly aloft by one of the officers, singing as they went. In a particular street, or on a particular bridge, they would stop and sing four or five hymns from their book, each verse being read over first by one of the officers. There was no 'sermonising', and seldom any prayers. The act itself was the act of witness.

It was both strange and easy to participate in this Friday night event; strange in the suddenness with which one found oneself in circumstances and surroundings so totally unusual, and easy in that almost every tune we sang was familiar and brought back memories of mission halls in Glasgow's East End, evangelistic campaigns, churches of the past, fellowship groups and so many other situations where the Gospel in its simplest form seemed relevant rather than suspect and the words of the Bible in all their grand familiarity felt much more penetrating than superficial contemporary philosophies that never reach the heights and depths of the human spirit's need. It is easy to ask what possible effect this routine, repeated over twenty-eight years every Friday night, could have on hardened city life and especially that for which the Red Light area stands. But who can tell what effect the chord of memory or aspiration, the mere sight and sound of dedicated people with no ulterior motives, can have on one who listens by the way? Bosshardt knows of some who having seen and heard these sounds, realised the wrong they were about to do, came to themselves, and like the prodigal, went home.

Bosshardt, talking to this one or that, friend or stranger, on the edge of the crowd would make some contact out there within the reality of a sort of modern Sodom and Gomorrha that a thousand sermons and a thousand lectures would not touch. The One who 'went about doing good' would see His reflection in this simple activity in the midst of the facts of life, and know that, 'in His name', the singers and the songs were there.

The march has only once had to be stopped in twenty-eight years because of opposition or obstruction. Otherwise, rain or shine, it has gone on – if wet, perhaps without the accordion, for obvious practical reasons.

The evening ended as it always does – with coffee and conversation in the Goodwill Centre and a count-up of the cash collected for *War Crys*.

Around twelve thirty I went to my simple room in Bosshardt's flat to await the development of my understanding of the work of witness and mercy centred on this extraordinary woman. The sounds from the streets and the clubs went on into the night, for the life of the Red Light area is a life that appreciates darkness rather than light.

As I lay ready to sleep I went back over the day, as is my custom, to see what had been done of use and to learn from what had been less worthwhile. I was now sure it was right to be here to see what Bosshardt was giving and doing in such an extraordinary place. For the rest, a long day was over and it was time to sleep.

But obviously not for Bosshardt.

2

Change Of Direction

I HAD BEEN asleep only a few minutes – or so it seemed – when I was awakened by a hammering on the door two floors below. It was in fact around three a.m. The music in the night club was still drifting across the moonlit canals. The hubbub of voices continued in the streets, still alive with pleasure-seekers.

I heard the light go on in the next-door room. Bosshardt was already responding to the cry for help that the knocking implied. It was far from abnormal for there to be such noise in the night. On the contrary, it was typical of the life this woman led; a life that could not be called her own, for she belonged, it seemed, to everyone.

The stairs responded to her footsteps – a squeak here, a rattle there. I heard the door from her flat to the Goodwill office open, then the unlocking of the larger main door onto the street. The voice of a woman, upset and irate, sounded in the distance. The door closed and I assumed the visitor was inside. She was, but so were her four children.

There had been an argument at home, the same old argument that had taken place many times. It always ended in threats – she must go; she would go; she would take the children with her, and so on. Tonight the threats had become reality. Tempers had been lost as rationality had disappeared. She had wakened the children, called a taxi and ordered the driver to the O. Z. Voorburgwal and the Goodwill Centre. It was Bosshardt's problem.

Bosshardt was used to such problems. How often her night's rest was broken into by just such alarums and excursions. There was always someone in need. And anyone in need in Amsterdam – and far beyond it too – knew that when they were thrown on the stormy seas of life, Bosshardt would be there to say 'Here is my hand.'

But the humanity that responds does not need to be a softness that colludes. Many a time, of course, Bosshardt had opened the door and said 'Come in.' There are always beds and buns and brews of tea or coffee for those with nowhere to go. It was her way of life not to think of herself, but to drive herself on for others. But softness was not the only characteristic of Bosshardt. She could be firm – for Christ's sake. Within a few minutes mother and family were back in their taxi, sharply despatched to where they ought to be – at home. If families had to be broken up, then let it be done in a civilised, sensitive way, not as a night-time drama, damaging to all concerned, including the children. There was no sense in snap solutions of this kind.

The taxi left to take them home. For a brief hour or two Bosshardt returned to bed.

What is this woman's background? How did this sacrificial way of life evolve?

It is not the purpose of this book (as I have already said) to analyse in psychological terms the make-up and motivation, conscious or unconscious, of this dramatic personality. All I shall do is tell the factual story of where she began and how her life has developed. 'By their fruits, ye shall know them.' It is what her life has produced that has brought blessing to thousands, and that is all that matters here. It is a record of her experience – the experience that is expressed in unstinted help, freely given.

You cannot argue with experience. All the philosophising in the world by Sadducee, Scribe, Pharisee or any of their contemporary counterparts is ineffective when faced by the authority of fact. 'I don't understand and can't argue with your profound academic learning,' the man who was born blind seems to say in the New Testament; but then goes on to produce the answer that no one can dispute: 'One thing I know: whereas I was blind, now I can see.' The call-girls and the outcasts of Amsterdam and elsewhere who have been at the receiving end of Bosshardt's outstretched hand won't brook any argument or listen to doctrinaire theories that pigeon-hole their Bosshardt as some psychological type whose life and work are 'explained' (or explained away) by technical jargon. They know her in whom they have believed and are persuaded about all she is able to say and do. They don't really care about the how and the why. It is the blessings that matter.

Alida Bosshardt was brought up in what she has described as 'an ordinary family'. Alida's grandparents on her father's side were members of the Dutch Reformed Church. Her father was one of a large family but five of them – all sisters – died when still young. Mr. Bosshardt, like the other sons, was given a business of his own, a grocery business in Utrecht. It was when he was serving as an assistant in Gouda that he met Alida's mother.

Mrs. Bosshardt did not come from a religious background, nor did she set any particular importance, apparently, on involvement in organised religion. But she had a faith, Alida felt. Mr. and Mrs. Bosshardt were married legally at the town hall as Dutch law required, but later in the day they had, as so many then did, a further marriage ceremony in church. There the marriage was dedicated and confirmed. So far as Alida knew, they were never in the church 'with the beautiful windows' again, though they did later have another look at the windows – from outside.

Two children were born of the marriage, Henk in 1910 and Alida on June 8th., 1913. There was also an adopted child, whom Alida always looked on as a brother (he was adopted before her birth). His name was Jan Pennings. Alida was baptised on August 3rd by the family minister, Dominee Woudstra.

Mr. Bosshardt had a very hard time in his business. Things didn't go well in that period – the twenties – so money was not at all plentiful. Mrs. Bosshardt was particularly conscious of the need for extreme thrift and, in her attitudes to money, influenced her daughter greatly. Mrs. Bosshardt, for example, simply refused to spend money she did not have. If shoes could not be afforded, no shoes were bought. If money for food did not exist, then watery porridge was provided.

This principle rubbed off completely on Alida and laid the basis that made it possible for her to accept without question or complaint lack of personal financial resources. The simple life she follows lacks comfort and luxury, and literal poverty, if this comes her way, is fully accepted. Her whole mode of life has been an illustration of the attitude to money she learned in her financially restricted childhood. Her life is, therefore, as comfortable as she would wish it but is simple and frugal by modern worldly standards. She still will not spend what she has not got and has applied that principle throughout her life and work.

By the time Alida was seven years old, the family business situation was very bad, and bankruptcy stared her father in the face. He had to find employment and so became a commercial traveller dealing in tea, coffee, beer and 'honey cakes'. Alida remembers the honey cakes well. While in retrospect she has some doubts about the morality of the exercise, she took part in doctoring somewhat dry honey cakes for sale the next day!

Mr. Bosshardt lost his job on Christmas Eve, 1925. Alida remembers still seeing him come home that evening with a crate of bottles of beer. He was quite elated about his consignment of drink, but Mrs. Bosshardt did not share his enthusiasm. The future, in the light of his dismissal, was on her mind. Though her father did have a slight streak of irresponsibility in him and her mother was much more disciplined, Alida doesn't recall family quarrels at all. Perhaps Mrs. Bosshardt's own parents helped the family to keep on a reasonably even keel, for they (Alida thinks) probably paid the rent of their pleasant house at Janskerkhof from time to time.

Another significant event involving her father happened in that year. He decided to join the Roman Catholic Church.

Why he took this step is not wholly clear, but Alida's mother thought it had something to do with his musical talents, which had not been used in his own Dutch Reformed Church. She doubted if he was a Roman Catholic at heart, but did not feel too anxious over the change. The fact his 'conversion' was expressed in a happier disposition and more family concern pleased her. His tendency to go out unannounced became a thing of the past and he seemed happy at home.

The Roman Catholic Church certainly recognised his gifts, for he became church organist there. For this he received one hundred guilders (the equivalent then of ten pounds) a year as an honorarium. That in fact was his first income after he lost his job. Later he joined the

Utrechtse Courant as a journalist. It was a Catholic newspaper and gave him a salary of two hundred and thirty guilders a month. The progress pleased Alida's mother greatly, especially as she had the security of receiving all his pay and controlling it. Generous man that he was (and perhaps Alida herself took over from him the willingness to give away all he had), he would without a thought, hand his only five-guilder piece to someone, so it was perhaps wiser that Mrs. Bosshardt should control it all in those difficult days! But Alida does recall that when she later joined The Salvation Army, he would send her five guilders with the plea not to tell her mother that he had done so. Mrs. Bosshardt felt that as Alida had joined the Army of her own accord, she should look after herself!

Alida's brother Henk was also anxious to become a journalist, a desire that did precipitate family tension. Mrs. Bosshardt was not always happy with the habits of the profession and complained if he came home a little the worse for drink. It wasn't that he drank heavily but Mrs. Bosshardt was always anxious about the money her husband spent in this way. Henk's desire to study for the journalistic profession, and her finding that a little rum, saved for a pudding, had been secretly consumed by him, created great anxiety for her. Only on the condition that he supported himself was Henk ultimately allowed to become a journalist.

Mr. Bosshardt's becoming a Catholic upset some of the relatives of the family. Mrs. Bosshardt reacted by developing more interest in the Dutch Reformed Church, perhaps partly because the attitude to families married in that Church was very basic to her. She would be loyal, at least, to their commitment. Alida meantime was growing up against a background of divided religious attachment and felt the problems of that tension. She attended a Protestant school but has told how she had to stay in after hours on a Monday if she had attended the Roman Catholic Church on Sunday.

It was perhaps out of division and out of divided loyalties to a disciplined mother and a less disciplined father who, nevertheless, took a major step in relation to his own fulfilment, that Alida herself developed her personal self-discipline. Alongside that there was the belief in her own intuition and conviction that led her to rebel against personal dissatisfaction with what she was doing and pushed her to 'launch out into the deep'. She was eleven when she did this in a dramatic way.

'I am leaving that school,' she said after another Monday punishment for going to the Roman Catholic Church on Sunday. Her father's response was, 'Please yourself, but don't say I gave you permission' (perhaps with an eye on the disapproving relatives). Mrs. Bosshardt wanted none of it, of course, but that afternoon Alida went to her teacher to ask for her 'small-pox certificate and her sports-gloves' as she was not coming back!

She didn't.

As Alida grew older, her sense of dissatisfaction with both the Churches represented by her parents became stronger. She disliked the Roman Catholic Church because of its use of Latin and her consequent lack of knowledge of what was going on in worship. The Dutch Reformed Church of her mother did not meet her own inner spiritual needs and searching. It was then that she was introduced to The Salvation Army. Her brother by adoption unwittingly played the crucial role in her discovery.

Jan and his girl friend had planned to go to a

Salvation Army service, but Jan fell ill and wasn't able to go. 'Zus' (Zus was Alida's pet name within the family circle) 'Zus,' the girl had said, 'would you like to come with me to the service?'

It was in that moment that a life's journey began – a journey that has led to national fame and respect for a disciple of Christ. 'Yes,' she said, 'I would.' That visit led to more visits to the Army's services and to Alida's reaching the point where the only way forward was through the welcoming doors of the Army.

For a time, Alida continued, for her mother's sake, to keep in touch with the Dutch Reformed Church. She became a teacher in the Sunday school, but still felt she did not want to be confirmed there. Inevitably the time came when she must choose the particular direction she must go – and that had to be in the direction of the Army. She had already told the Roman Catholic priest of her decision. She had questioned him about the right of the Roman Catholic Church to claim sole or total authority in spiritual things. He had ended by telling her that if she really wanted to go to the Army, he could not stop her. The Dutch Reformed Church minister was understanding. Alida quotes his reply: 'The Army is washing the dirty linen and the Church is there to dry it. If you insist, I will phone your parents and you will be able to go. As long as you are honest enough to come back if you are disappointed, what does it matter?'

Alida Bosshardt has not been disappointed and has never needed to go back to one whom she describes as 'a fine, understanding man'. Nor would he expect her, in the light of all that has happened, to have done so.

The change of direction was complete.

The journey that mattered had begun.

3

The Evolution Of A Mission

ALIDA BOSSHARDT WAS eighteen when (as she says) she 'consciously committed herself to God' and saw that commitment being worked out through The Salvation Army. Asked at her enrolment service if she 'claimed salvation' and if she, of her own free will, wanted to become a soldier of The Salvation Army, she confirmed that this was so. 'Here is my hand,' she seemed to say as a sign and seal of this decision as she raised her right hand to symbolise her commitment. 'Here is my hand,' she has said to countless people in trouble ever since. So in 1933 she became a Salvationist in Utrecht I Corps.

Her father bought her uniform and bonnet. That bonnet (for she still wears the 'old-fashioned' one now often replaced by the more modern version) was crucially important for her. When a friend asked to accompany her on her work in order to see her in action and suggested it would be easier if she wore a Salvation Army hat too, Alida would not have it. 'It is not just any hat,' she said.

There is probably no uniform on earth that is more respected than The Salvation Army uniform. It is a passport and a protection. It will take its wearer into pub and prison, club and casino, brothel and bar. It will protect the soldier in a hostile crowd, for none will treat it with disrespect. It is honoured – as it is an honour to wear it. But for the first time? Bosshardt, like every other new recruit no doubt, felt rather strange! She says that it was with 'mixed feelings of disquiet and vanity' that she first showed herself in public. It had its advantages. People felt free to ask about the uniform where they might have been reluctant to ask about the person inside it. It opens the door to confidences being shared, sins being confessed, pain being expressed. It stands for trust and honesty, for acceptance and kindness, for dedication and commitment. Alida Bosshardt found that, young girl that she was, she was being told of private secrets, hidden relationships, faults and failings by people old enough to be her mother. She prayed with those who had unburdened their hearts – not that she found this easy, for it wasn't – because inner conviction and prompting told her that this is what she must do. Not to do it would feel like a denial of her faith.

The pressure on Alida not to go forward to full service in the Army continued – especially from her father. He did his best to persuade her to leave the Army, to leave off her uniform. He suggested she should have a talk with his bishop and made an appointment for her. This she kept. Deliberately, but unknown to her father, she took a Salvation Army collecting box with her under her cape. The interview was a waste of time – or perhaps not. She was still a Salvationist and her collecting box was considerably heavier after the appointment!

Alida's mother also expected her to go back on her decision to join the Army, and kept a little room ready at home for her. It was never needed – in that sense. Those who know Bosshardt now know why such a turning back could never come. Indeed the calling she had undertaken was to her exciting and rewarding. 'Heavy?' she said to someone who asked her about the 'heavy' burden she had undertaken. 'It's not heavy for me.' She truly has found, and says it vehemently still, that His burden is light, though in sheer hard fact it has meant self-denial, poverty, physical strain and demands almost beyond anyone's endurance. It has meant scrubbing floors and clearing up other people's mess. It has meant conducting the funeral of a mother, eleven of whose twelve children she had brought into this world. It has meant constantly dealing with the drunks and the derelicts of human society at any hour of day or night. It has meant walking in the rain selling *War Crys* to people in nice houses; cycling miles and miles to stop and deliver her papers. It has meant living with the sin and evil of this world to the point of descending into other people's hells. It has meant (as it did for ten years) sleeping behind a curtain in a ward with fifteen boys, with no privacy at all and only a small chest-of-drawers with a wash-basin on top as furniture. The wardrobe had to be shared with two or three other officers. But at no time did Alida, having set her hand to the plough, look back. 'I sometimes found it difficult to have nothing of my own, no house of my own, never to be able to put my legs under my own table,' she writes. But she continues: 'If you haven't much to lose, you haven't much to look after.'

It was with that degree of dedication that as the young committed soldier, she decided to try to train as an officer, not because of personal ambition (if that word has any relevance in The Salvation Army context) but because she felt the Lord intended her to be just that, for to be an officer meant a full-time commitment, and she felt wholly committed. She did not find that part of her preparation easy. Essentially a practical, active enthusiast, happy running errands of mercy and helping people in trouble, she found no need to know and care about how, when and where the Kings of Israel and Judah reigned. Her first examination result was so bad that she thought she would be sent home to do some basic study before continuing. (The only other time she nearly had to leave the Army was when she fell asleep during a meeting – she says from fatigue and boredom. A very angry Colonel told her it was no way for a young officer to behave and that she would be given 'a last chance' to show her dedication!)

However bad at theory, in practical work Alida Bosshardt shone. Her Chief, the Commissioner, saw her gifts clearly and had great hopes of this outstanding young officer. Should it be field and corps work or should she specialise in social work? The decision turned out to be that she would serve in Corps II in Rotterdam.

Cadet Lieutenant Bosshardt, as she had now become, was taught in the Army that you learn to give completely and not expect anything back in return. She knows that is true and acts on it totally. It means that her life must be one of 'ups and downs' – which is what it has been. But Alida was saved by two crucial qualities. One was – and is – her total dedication and the other has been her sense of humour. The first is what the whole of this book is about. The second is always likely to break through in the most solemn situations. As a child, she was the tomboy, up to all kinds of tricks and fun. As the young officer, she fought a constant battle with her bonnet which was always lopsided. To ensure that her bonnet was smart, she polished its straw crown before going on parade. But the rains came, and the winds blew and beat upon that bonnet and Cadet-Lieut. Bosshardt became bluer with every step as whatever she used melted along the way!

Bosshardt always wears her uniform, so theatre visits (a rare luxury) are likewise uniform occasions. She says: 'When you go to the theatre in uniform, and you go to the Ladies, what does the attendant say? "You cannot sell any *War Crys* here. Please keep that in mind." '

The years up to 1940 were difficult years. Unemployment and poverty were rife, and the Army had to decide where it could give most help. Bosshardt was allocated the care of eighty children in the Social Homes, and in that work she found scope for the childlike part of her nature. She not only looked after but played with the children.

In 1938 Lieutenant Bosshardt became Captain Bosshardt, and it was in her period as Captain that she had to face all the problems of an 'underground' movement. With the collapse of the Netherlands in 1940, The Salvation Army was virtually liquidated. Continuation of the work in any kind of official way was impossible in Nazi-controlled Holland, but so far as it was possible, caring went on, unofficially. The children were moved to several homes close together in the Residastraat in Amsterdam, but in July 1943 Allied attacks on the city killed and injured many. Bosshardt and the children survived, but it was essential that they move out of Amsterdam at once. She took all the children to the Central Station and boarded a train for Hilversum. Once there, she made straight for the Army's hall and kept them in it for the night. There she called on the help of her brother, Henk, to find her temporary accommodation, but it had in fact become a time for constant moving on. With extraordinary energy and initiative, she moved the children from one place to another, constantly looking for possible new places in which they might stay. She was arrested by German soldiers and had to prove what she was doing. It was a time for courage, strength and dedication. Bosshardt showed them all to an astonishing degree.

For Cadet-Lieutenant Bosshardt, the appointment to Rotterdam was another milepost in the evolution of a mission, a mission that was to take her in due course to share the life of the prostitutes of the Red Light area, to know fame through a 'This is Your Life' television programme, to meet with and share the life of the Dutch royal family, to create the Goodwill Centre as it is today, as well as the nearby hostels in that district, to witness through lecture, sermon, conversation, service and sacrifice to her faith and to create the fine new homes for old people in Amsterdam, opened as The Goodwillburgh as recently as 1975.

The entry in her girlhood diary, at the time of her first year of service as an officer, sums up her own view of her commitment:

All my days and all my hours,
All my will and all my powers,
All the passion of my soul,
Not a fragment, but the whole
  Shall be Thine, dear Lord.

4

Goodwill Among Men . . . and Women

ALIDA BOSSHARDT'S NATIONAL and international fame has very much focused on her work in the Red Light area; understandably, perhaps, for it is one of the sad weaknesses of the media in the latter part of the twentieth century that they must concentrate on the sensational aspects of life, however crude. As sex and sexual matters always carry the possibility of sensation in them, the particular ministry Bosshardt has exercised to the girls has been and is inevitably media material. On innumerable occasions, that ministry has received all the attention. It is in fact but a specialist part, given the particular sociological feature of the area, of a far wider and greater section of the social work carried out from the Goodwill Centre. It is that Goodwill Centre and all it stands for that is not only the ground of Bosshardt's special place in Dutch life, but the epitome of all Bosshardt is.

I shall have to return with emphasis to this point and try to ensure that Bosshardt is seen and remembered as The Salvation Army in all its witness, spiritual and social, in the centre of Amsterdam. The emphasis I shall put on the particular section of it that has focused on work with prostitutes is not intended to classify it as the whole of Bosshardt's ministry. Factually it isn't, for she is a Salvationist primarily and a social worker secondarily and the latter only as the outreach inherent in the Gospel. The important aspect of her particular work with prostitutes, as a Salvationist and as a trained social worker, is that she must be one of the few to have specialised in this way and it may help others called to a similar ministry (as our times will increasingly make necessary) to learn of her experience and attitudes. For this reason it must have a major place in this book. It is therefore true to say that, in the total ministry, spiritual and social, she has effected in Amsterdam, she is the embodiment of goodwill among men – and, for particular reasons, among women too.

With the war over, Captain Bosshardt was back at Headquarters in Amsterdam. There she provided social services for all – providing clothes, financial help, advice; giving consultations to anyone in need. And there were many problems in post-war Holland. The Headquarters themselves could not possibly be a social work agency. Their function was administrative, so Bosshardt, working in the Women's Social Department, became the point of reference for everyone arriving at Headquarters believing they would get help of some kind. Receptionist, caretakers, and all the other officers found it best to act in the same way. 'Send them to Bosshardt.'

Bosshardt did not object. She much preferred working with people to administration. She found she had the ability to talk to them, no matter what their level. She understood them, and they found something special in her, so she accepted her role with enthusiasm. Her work began to develop outside office hours as she took clothes to a newly-born child and a poor mother, or went on some other kind of mercy mission, if only to say 'Here is my hand!'

It was obvious however that an evolution of Bosshardt's mission in life was rapidly taking place. She had no appointment to this particular work. It was growing around her and she was growing into it. Surely this was the Lord's doing, she felt. And it really was marvellous.

For three years and more the work developed. More and more people came for help and, as the news of the service spread, more and more people made contributions to it. They brought clothes, money, food. A toilet became a store cupboard. Telephone calls reached a huge figure, as Bosshardt, conscious of her lack of formal social work training, sought help from others – from the Red Cross for example.

Strangely enough no social service work had ever been set up in the inner city. In Amsterdam North and in the southern part as well as in the Jordaan, there was organised goodwill work of this kind. Now in the inner city, the demand for it was overwhelming. And it was clear to all that the only person to set this up was Bosshardt. She already represented 'goodwill' in the inner city.

The next step was the purchase by Headquarters of a small house in the Nieuwe Brugsteeg, because the Reclamation Department was short of space. The basement was not in use, so Bosshardt was allowed this for her people in need.

1948 was for Bosshardt a vintage year, vintage in that it seemed to demonstrate the way in which her mission was to be expressed. She became Senior Captain and was given responsibility for all goodwill work in Holland. At the same time, Headquarters decided to set up Goodwill Work in the inner city, work that must be both spiritual and social. How close that was to the famous dictum of William Booth that has for ever characterised the impact of The Salvation Army in such spectacular ways. 'Soup, soap and salvation' he had said. This was what that part of his world-wide Army in the Netherlands was specifically laying down for the inner city of Amsterdam. Booth, whose books are in the bookcase in Bosshardt's own room in the flat at the Goodwill Centre, would have been proud of his Dutch Senior Captain and would have seen in her the very incarnation of his intuition and instruction. And she, I am sure, would have sensed his approval.

Bosshardt was officially appointed to that work and so began the quarter of a century and more of the extraordinary piece of Christian service and witness in the heart of old Amsterdam, from which, officially, she retires in June 1978.

Bosshardt installed her little office in the basement as a temporary home until the right place for the work could be discovered. She found it in 1951 – the oldest brick-built house in Amsterdam. It was built by a rich ship-owner in 1581 and first occupied in 1600. Known as D'Leuwenburgh, its official address is Oudezijds, Voorburgwal 14.

With one hundred guilders, an Army flag and the blessing of the Lord given by Headquarters, Bosshardt began her ministry. The Goodwill Work had to be self-supporting financially and Bosshardt knew that responsibility lay squarely on her. For the first ten years, she was on her own. She slept in the office on a mattress and with some blankets given her by an Amsterdam hospital. During the day, when the office was in use, blankets and mattress had to be stuffed in a toilet.

Because her bedroom by night was the office by day, it was literally impossible for her to be ill. Another room meant more rent and this simply could not be afforded.

Throughout the operation at the Goodwill Centre, the sale of *War Crys* has been a crucial factor. The annual sale runs to around eighty thousand copies, bringing in an income of sixty-five thousand guilders a year for the Centre. *War Cry* has a double purpose – the proclamation of its message and the income that it brings.

The primary task of The Salvation Army is the preaching of the Gospel under the slogan:

Christ for the world, the world for Christ.

The Goodwill Centre represents that and carries it out. But it adds as its aim:

The Gospel in Word and *Deed*.

It is in the 'doing' that perhaps The Salvation Army so outstrips the mainstream churches. Its social work and its skill in dealing with the lower levels of human existence have characterised its history and won it universal respect. In the centre of Amsterdam these deeds are expressed in the hostels I saw on that first night I spent in the Red Light area, in the Ruytenburgh where evangelical and pastoral work is done, at meetings on Sundays where the Gospel is preached, in a Sunday school for children of the district, in a club for the over-sixties, youth clubs and women's organisations. The premises allow for emergency shelter for women and girls in special need. The Gastenburgh is the sitting-room for the district. It was there I first found Sister Henny on duty on that night I arrived. The club is open every day from eight thirty a.m. to five thirty p.m. and from seven p.m. to ten thirty p.m. There is no entrance fee. All are welcome at the coffee-counter, in the T.V. room, in the lounge, etc. A social worker is present on weekdays to help people with personal problems. Shelter is provided for men who have nowhere to go.

Perhaps these few paragraphs bear out the total nature and extent of the Goodwill work that Bosshardt creates and supervises. It is a ministry of consistency and competence to all in need in a community of thirty thousand people, of which four thousand are aged and three thousand young. Within it, as I have said, the special problems of the prostitute must have attention because thousands practise the profession within this concentrated area. And it is that fact that brings such a huge number of people into the area, multiplying the problems, adding to the victims, subtracting from that which is 'good and lovely and of good report', and creating divisions of a kind not met in 'ordinary' communities.

In 1958, Bosshardt undertook special training to help her with her ministry. From that time till 1961 she studied for a social work diploma, thus adding skills to dedication and knowledge to commitment.

So for the thirty years that end now, the evolution of this remarkable mission has continued entirely through the unique contribution of this woman. Her strength, skill, sensitivity and sincerity, along with her faith, her love and hope have brought the true Light into the area of the Red Light; have brought the One who came not to condemn the world but to save it, to a place where salvation is so urgent. Perhaps Bosshardt has understood that more than most for the thrust of her ministry is, some may feel surprisingly, not to condemn – for there seems much to condemn – but to offer salvation within the situation.

We shall return to that thought in some depth in due course. For the moment, we turn to two extraordinary events that elevated 'the envoy of the Lord' to national recognition.

5

This Is Your Life!

ON FEBRUARY 19th, 1959, 'the Major', as she had now both become and become known, under pressure from friends agreed to attend a lecture given by a certain Colonel Crok. Just before she was due to leave, however, she realised that all her workers were off that evening and she simply dare not leave the Goodwill Centre unstaffed. She rang her friend and colleague, Major Werkman, to give her apologies. Embarrassed and anxious, Major Werkman appealed to her to make some urgent re-arrangement, as a surprise had been planned for her by her colleagues. If she did not turn up, they would be very disappointed indeed. As always, Bosshardt hated disappointing anyone, so she made arrangements to go.

In the Lecture Hall in Laren, there had been frenzied activity preparing for that month's edition of '*Anders dan Anderen*' or as we know it in Britain, 'This is Your Life'. The subject chosen was, of course, Major Bosshardt. Everyone knew that if the Major had realised what was planned, she just would not have been there! Indeed to the very last moment, there was acute anxiety as to whether she would arrive at all, for if she met someone in trouble on the way she would forget the lecture altogether.

The programme director was also anxious on other grounds. As always, there was the uncertainty of how people would react and there was some apprehension about the specific area of work in which the Major was involved. How would viewers react to the national publicity given to the Red Light area? It was all right to have it tucked away in a corner of the big city where people could do what they liked anonymously. But mass projection of the trade in lust and carnal commercialism would be less comfortable. The area had not had this sort of exposure before ... and of course the programme was 'family viewing.'* There was then an element of professional risk in the programme, but Director Bert Garthoff believed deeply the subject was right and the risk must be taken.

The Major arrived in the dimly lit hall, and was shepherded to her reserved seat. She whispered 'Good evening' to the man next to her, a 'Good evening' in fact heard throughout the Netherlands. Garthoff and his camera crew were already in action. 'Major Bosshardt, this is your life.' Wholly taken aback, the Major quickly responded 'in character' – as she had done when she slipped her collecting box under her uniform on the way to the appointment with the bishop. There was so much she needed for the Centre. It was an opportunity. They were actually saying to her, 'Major Bosshardt, come and tell us what you need for your Centre, for we know you need many things.' She was on the stage at once. 'I need a new hall,' she said.

So the programme that led to a huge step forward in the evolution of her Centre – and her personal mission – was under way. They showed film, shot without her knowledge, of the Centre and of her colleagues, colleagues who had willingly co-operated for the sake of the Major. They highlighted the district she called home, the girls who were part of her family, the clubs into which she was always free to go, the old women and men in her hostels and the Centre itself, heartbeat of the mission.

*We will discuss later how exposure to pornography does or does not affect children, as seen by Sister Henny in relation to her own family.

Journalist Jo Manassen told of the night she was at the Centre when children who had run away from an institution arrived at the door seeking a refuge. She added that the Major's voice is husky because of her constant lack of sleep. There was film of the annual Christmas dinner at the Centre. Immediately and spontaneously, after initial nervousness, Bosshardt gave a running commentary on the whole event. She spoke of the multitude of lonely people in Amsterdam, those who have no one with whom to share troubles – or joys. She reminded those who have and take for granted, of those who haven't and would cherish what we regard as natural.

People who had been converted through her ministry paid tribute to her influence. Women now happily married and with families gave their thanks for the change that came after she had crossed their paths. The area doctor, Dr. Ronner, with sly but affectionate humour, commented that the Major 'is not an American beauty, but she possesses something that others do not possess', a willingness to be bound up with humanity and to be with people in need, to sit where they sit in their pain, fear, distress and loneliness.

A boy from Korea who had arrived in Amsterdam with no knowledge of Dutch thanked her for all she had done for him. 'She reared me,' he said. A relative talked of the quality of her private life and added with a smile: 'It's nice to have the chance to talk to you tonight. You never have time otherwise!'

One after another came, invited to pay their tribute, happy to give their thanks. Meantime, off-stage, the studio switchboard was being jammed with calls. The interviewer broke in to say that viewers were offering a mass of gifts to help her work – blankets and more blankets, a vacuum cleaner, linen of every kind, coffee sets, tea sets, a year's supply of soap, one hundred children's books, and so on, and so on. Another interruption by the interviewer was to say that all the building material that she needed would be given free to her by a firm of suppliers. Another offered two hundred and fifty kilos of paint. Another offered a free cigar to everyone coming to the opening of the new hall (even if Booth might have turned in his grave over that offer!) A removal firm offered its services completely free of charge. The interviewer broke in again: 'Major Bosshardt, what is your giro number? People want to send you money.'

The programme almost became sheer chaos as right across the country the impact of Bosshardt was felt. Never in the experience of the producer had there been a reaction quite like this. 'You ought to have St. Paul on your programme,' someone had once said to him, the interviewer told the audience. 'Tonight it feels as if just that had happened,' he added, moved by his own involvement with the contemporary apostle to the nation.

That programme made it possible for a dream to become a reality, for Bosshardt's vision to be incarnate in buildings, equipment and people. Perhaps she has always tried to do it all by herself – not for ambition's sake, but perhaps because she underestimates her own value and cannot always see why others might want to help her. Through 'This is Your Life', an army of helpers became involved and lifted her over the boundaries that an individual effort must have, however great the talent, however outstanding the courage, however deep the faith. 'You can't do it all yourself,' said Jethro to Moses. 'Choose people to help you.' So he chose his elders. Jesus needed his twelve. Bosshardt has always had her helpers but she is essentially a remarkable individualist who has carried a cause on her back. 'This is Your Life' let hundreds come over and help – for a moment at least, and in a crucial way.

As a direct result of the programme, the Ruytenburgh, the spiritual-pastoral centre mentioned earlier, was opened on April 14th, 1962. It was a well-known inner city building dating back to 1500. From 1500 to 1576 a grocer is said to have lived in the house. It has been suggested that the family changed their name to Ruytenburgh. If so, the connection has historical interest in that a great-grandson became a lieutenant in the Fleet and appears on the famous Rembrandt painting 'Nightwatch', standing next to Captain Frans Bonnink Cocq. A reproduction of the painting can still be seen in the Goodwill Centre.

The Ruytenburgh had become quite derelict, so the Army had first to buy the premises for eighteen thousand pounds, then spend a considerable amount of money on renovation. It is now a pleasing meeting hall with halls and rooms for clubs and gatherings. Once again it buzzes with people and action. The famous and the unknown meet within its walls and the work of the Lord progresses within it and around it. The poor are helped, the lonely befriended, the sick are received, the ill are cared for, the homeless find a place to rest, the Gospel is proclaimed in words and deeds.

When the Ruytenburgh was opened, the whole street shared in the joy. The girls had a day off.* Even their employers (for employers they usually have), ceased trading for the day. The flags were put out, the street decorated. This would be the centre of the social work, leaving the Goodwill Centre itself for administrative purposes. For Bosshardt, this was indeed the day of triumph.

*It is hard for those on the outside to think of the prostitute's profession as 'work' or 'employment' from which, as with everyone else's work situations, holidays and days off are relevant. We shall return to this point.

It was also the occasion for her to be awarded the title O.F. – Order of the Founder. It is the highest honour The Salvation Army can give. It was presented to her, after an address by Lieut. Commissioner Wm. Palstra, by Mrs. Colonel Holland who pinned the decoration on to her beloved uniform in the name of all the women officers of The Salvation Army.

'Please tell the General, I shall do my best in the future and not to worry about me,' said the Major.

She has done so, for just to do that is her life – in His name.

But the programme led to a further fascinating occasion, indeed a right royal one.

6

A Royal Occasion

IT WAS AFTER 'This is Your Life' that an invitation came to Bosshardt to meet Queen Juliana. In 1960, when the Queen spent three days at the Royal Palace in Amsterdam, she invited several people to come and talk to her about their work. One was a priest, another represented a particular youth club and the third was Colonel Bosshardt.

Officially intended to be a twenty-minute visit, the conversation, over a cup of tea, ran on much longer. Queen Juliana questioned Bosshardt closely on her work and made a link with her that has remained real ever since.

But the royal occasion that hit the headlines involved not Queen Juliana, but her daughter Princess Beatrix, for it involved an adventure with her that caught the imagination of press and public alike.

Princess Beatrix was very anxious to meet and mix with 'ordinary people'. But she also had a particular respect and affection for The Salvation Army. In most situations she had to stay within her role as Princess, but she felt when she was with the Army, as she had been on occasion, that she was among real friends, and could be spontaneous and natural.

Bosshardt had met the Princess on a number of occasions – at a lecture in Leiden when she was studying there, at a wedding reception and at other official functions. Beatrix had said to Bosshardt on one occasion: 'The work of The Salvation Army intrigues me. Could I possibly come with you on a tour of your district?' 'Of course,' Bosshardt had replied, 'you are more than welcome. It is not, in any way, a problem for me. So long as you are happy to do it, it is all right.' So in 1965 Princess Beatrix arranged to tour the inner city area with Bosshardt.

Though Bosshardt had said there was no problem about the arrangement, there were in fact some practical difficulties. All invitations to the royal family had to go through National Headquarters, just as radio and T.V. appearances and the writing of books also had to have official approval. Bosshardt did not, however, really want to ask permission in this case or make what was really an informal arrangement an official visit. In any case, it was highly important that the press and the media should not get to know what was happening, or the whole point of the operation would be destroyed.

One of the reasons for the Army's rule that invitations must go through Headquarters was to avoid too many requests and possibly even different plans being made at exactly the same time. Suppose they had plans to invite Princess Beatrix to some national event in the near future. That in itself would kill the informal visit she planned. Bosshardt the individualist and enthusiast was concerned as to how the Army, in a responsible official capacity, would react. What about security? If the royal visitor was recognised, might there be resentment to the point of violence, at her intrusion into private places? What would the Dutch public think of their Princess visiting the kind of places that abound in its Red Light area? Would there be criticism of the Army for involving a member of the royal family in such an exploit?

Nor was the visit to be one made to 'nice' places and show-piece situations on the customary royal style. The whole operation was pointless if Beatrix did not see the reality, sordid and sinful as it was, and it certainly was her own wish to see the work Bosshardt did in authentic situations.

The Commissioner was not wholly in favour of the escapade, but Bosshardt felt it impossible to write to the Princess and say that the projected visit could not happen. It was then that Princess Irene decided to become a Roman Catholic. Bosshardt decided the royal family had enough on their hands, so did nothing more about it.

In September, Princess Beatrix rang Bosshardt at the Centre. 'What has happened to my invitation?' she asked. Bosshardt told her the Army officially was not happy at the projected visit, and could agree to it only if she took the initiative. Obviously the Princess too was not finding royal officialdom very sympathetic to the visit. That was why she had hoped Bosshardt would invite her! 'That shows you aren't allowed everything *you* want,' said Bosshardt jokingly over the phone to Beatrix. It was left that Bosshardt would hear further from the Princess in due course.

In January of the following year, 1966, Bosshardt had a call from Professor Schipper, President of the National Council of Social Service. He told Bosshardt that the Princess was busy for some time – a few months probably – with the work of the Council. She was to visit a Children's Home and an Eventide complex, talk to social workers, visit the centre for 'telephone counselling', and be a member of a committee studying the sociology of the contemporary situation. But she also wanted to see something of the work of The Salvation Army, preferably in the inner city of Amsterdam. This put the problem firmly into the court of Professor Schipper who rang to get Bosshardt's advice, knowing there was anxiety over the project.

Bosshardt passed the buck to her Commissioner, Commissioner Palstra, and suggested Schipper should ring him. She was still ambivalent about the idea – keen that Beatrix should see the area and particularly what The Salvation Army was doing in it, but nervous lest anything should go wrong. She could see possible consequences to the visit, but what she did not foresee was that it would become world news.

Finally Professor Schipper and Commissioner Palstra agreed the visit had to take place, and that the National Council for Social Service must be responsible for it, even though they were not too happy about it. If the attempt to meet the Princess's wishes was not met, she was obviously so determined that she might attempt to carry it out in some less official way.

So the tour was arranged. The Princess instructed that there must not be extra people involved in it. 'Everything must be as it always is. All I want to do is spend an afternoon and evening in and around the Goodwill Centre and see what you do.'

Bosshardt decided not to make any detailed plans in advance. The Princess would come at two thirty on Wednesday and from there on, the tour would evolve naturally and, in Bosshardt's terms, normally. But the news of the visit 'broke' – with complicated consequences.

How did news of the visit get out? Did even that happen? Was it just a coincidence that gave the world's press knowledge of the Princess's tour? Many press scoops happen just because someone with a camera or a notebook happens to be there at the right time. It seems that just that is the true explanation of the leak.

Peter Zonneveld, a photographer, did not know the Princess was coming to the Red Light area that day. What was a fact was that he was due to be married next day and so dropped in at the Hoppe pub for a drink with friends. The Hoppe pub was one of the places Bosshardt had in mind to take Princess Beatrix.

The Princess had arrived on time and unnoticed at the Goodwill Centre. She looked round the ground-floor office where each day the work of administering the service and mission goes on. It was the same office to which I had returned at midnight on my first Friday in Amsterdam, to share the traditional end of the witness walk – coffee after the Friday night singing in the streets. There, totally unnoticed, the Princess had watered the plants and made coffee for herself and some staff members. Bosshardt recalls that she used 'instant' coffee as she 'wasn't too good at this kind of thing'. She served her coffee also to Paul, a tramp who dropped in at the Centre, to Auntie Riek and to a police constable who looked in to ask some questions about a particular 'customer'.

At four thirty she climbed the winding staircase that leads up to Bosshardt's own flat. There she and Bosshardt had a cup of tea and talked, surrounded by the books of William Booth, pictures of prostitutes and children she had helped, letters and papers relating to the work (for this was her personal 'control centre'), the texts on the wall, and her few personal possessions.

As the tea progressed, some of the social workers joined in and the Princess was able to ask about the needs of the district, the nature of the families there, the housing problems, etc. Around five thirty Bosshardt served soup and bread, then spent some time reading the Bible with Princess Beatrix and in prayer before discussing spiritual matters of mutual concern. By this time, the inevitable nervousness of a strange and unusual situation had gone, and Beatrix had now become what so many others to whom Bosshardt talked had been – someone anxious to know about life itself and the problems life brings.

'What would you like to do then?' asked Bosshardt. 'What particularly would you like to see?'

'I would simply like to tour the district, see houses in poor condition where large families live, see old people and the conditions some of them face, and really just go where you would normally go.'

'Would you like to see our children's choir?' asked Bosshardt. 'Well,' replied the Princess, 'I have seen more children's choirs than I like to remember! But if you would like me to come, of course I will.'

'I have arranged for one of the children to give you a bunch of violets,' said Bosshardt, who was, in simple things, not always as subtle as in bigger things. 'Oh, no,' said Princess Beatrix, 'the children will go home and say what has happened, and the news is out.' Bosshardt handed over the violets herself.

The Princess decided to change her clothes for the tour. She had brought a coat, skirt and raincoat (not a particularly respectable one) as well as a wig and head-scarf. The 'dressing-up' caused lots of fun and laughter in Bosshardt's living-room as both struggled to get the disguise perfect.

It was raining a little as Princess Beatrix and Bosshardt set off down the Voorburgwal, arm in arm.

The first call was in the Koestraat, at a house where husband, wife and their five children lived in a two-roomed flat. 'This lady is interested in bad housing conditions here,' said Bosshardt to Marietje, the wife, who showed the visitor round the flat, especially indicating where each of the seven in the household slept. As it happened, the children were all there, and Princess Beatrix sat with them as Bosshardt did what she would always do, read to them from the Children's Bible.

The next call was on a family with six children. They all lived in one room, but as it happened, that very week they had acquired a second room in the upper part of the building. 'Would you like to see that room?' asked the woman. 'Yes, please,' said Bosshardt. 'Well, Major, you had better be careful on the stairs. They are not easy. The lady with you will be all right, for she is young.'

Before Bosshardt and the Princess left that home, it was the latter who read from the Children's Bible, while Bosshardt said the prayers for them. All talked together for some time before they left. None of them knew a princess had been with them.

After a call on one aged couple, Bosshardt and Beatrix made for the pubs and brothels. At the first pub – which also had a saloon and a boarding house – admission was, unusually, refused. 'They must have had a difficult day,' said Bosshardt, 'I always get in there.' (On the next visit Bosshardt paid to that pub, the woman was quite upset that she had refused entry, especially knowing then that her guest was Princess Beatrix!)

Princess Beatrix was not at all disturbed. What surprised her was that everyone else without exception, admitted them at once – as people universally did to Bosshardt. They talked with many of the girls, listened to their stories, talked about why they were involved in this work. The reasons were numerous – a child to maintain, the lack of the courage to get out, the chance to pick up easy money. The Princess talked easily with them and was wholly accepted by them as Bosshardt's friend.

The tour of the pubs and clubs went on. Bosshardt wanted to take the Princess to some of the busier pubs, so in de Voetboogsteeg they called at two pubs next to each other and linked by a communicating door. They sat at the bar and talked. 'This is an unusual evening for you to come,' said one client to Bosshardt. 'You usually come on Saturday evening.' 'That's true,' said Bosshardt, 'but we had some *War Crys* left and I didn't want to bring the same ones on Saturday. I have also brought someone with me who wants to learn about our work. To do that on Saturday is not easy when it is so crowded.'

The landlord was in a talkative mood and discussed many subjects. To Princess Beatrix he said: 'Why do you want to know about this work?' Someone else asked her if she was going to join the Army. 'I am not sure about that,' she replied. 'I shall have to give it a lot of thought. I really just wanted to know how the Army operates. This is my first evening out with them.'

Perhaps the biggest test came with the selling of *War Cry*. Where two are selling *War Crys* together, one goes to the back literally to be seen and recognised. Princess Beatrix took her supply of *War Crys* and approached one after another saying, 'Do you want the *Strijdkreet*?' When one was bought, she would always add: 'Make sure you read it.'

One client commented to the Princess: 'Sister, *you* only ask for a quarter (twenty-five cents) but the price is forty-five cents.' 'I'm sorry,' she replied. 'This is my first night with the Major.' 'The Major will tell you off if you don't ask enough, Sister,' came the reply. 'Perhaps the Major will forgive me on my first night,' said Princess Beatrix.

Bosshardt had in fact forgotten to tell her the price to ask, but there were other queries and questions on which no advance instruction would have been possible. 'Can I take you out for an evening?' 'Pity you are joining the Army – a nice girl like you.' 'Can we celebrate the Queen's birthday tomorrow together?'

Princess Beatrix parried all the questions easily and

without offence. 'I don't know what I am doing tomorrow. I have just started working for the Major,' she said to one questioner. Later she told Bosshardt how freely and easily people had spoken to her and she with them. To be part of the Army seemed to remove all kinds of barriers.

Bosshardt decided next to take her to the Hoppe pub. Perhaps this was a mistake, friends and colleagues told her later, but she thought it would be useful to visit a crowded, popular pub.

Bosshardt and Princess Beatrix entered the pub and, as arranged, Bosshardt went to the back. As it is a long, narrow place, Bosshardt was less able to control what was happening to the Princess. As they drew nearer to each other, Bosshardt became aware of a man she knew as Nico Koster. His mother had an embroidery shop and often gave items to the Centre's sale of work. With him was a man she didn't know, who was in fact Peter Zonneveld. Bosshardt noticed the two men set down their pints of beer, looking at each other somewhat significantly. She suspected they had guessed the secret and wondered what they would do. Peter Zonneveld disappeared outside. She was sure he had gone for his camera.

Bosshardt and the Princess had not, in fact, discussed what they would do if someone recognised Beatrix, nor had they thought at all of the possibility of a photograph being taken. For a moment, she became afraid. Assassination and similar acts of violence did happen. Could such a thing happen now? Peter Zonneveld appeared again, armed with his camera. Bosshardt hurried to the Princess and said: 'Come quickly, we must finish here at once!' 'Not yet,' said the Princess, 'I haven't covered everyone.' 'It doesn't matter. I will see them on Saturday,' replied Bosshardt. 'We *must* go now.' Beatrix saw Peter Zonneveld and his camera and understood why. She knew he was always trying to get pictures of her, and she knew that he knew her well by sight.

Bosshardt took the Princess by the arm and they left by a side-door. She did not want pictures taken in the Hoppe, or with other people there. Inevitably the headlines would be 'Princess in pub with criminals' or something like that.

Once outside, Bosshardt felt anxious to end the tour. 'The photographers won't leave us alone for sure,' she said. 'No,' said Princess Beatrix, 'we must complete the tour tonight, for it will never be possible again. The opportunity will be lost for ever.' Bosshardt liked that answer. They would go on.

Inside the Hoppe, an argument was going on between Peter Zonneveld and the landlord. The latter was adamant that no pictures must be taken inside. Peter Zonneveld argued angrily back. 'Don't you realise that was Princess Beatrix with Bosshardt?' he asked. 'You must be crazy,' said the by-standers. 'Don't get excited,' said the landlord. 'They left by a side-door some time ago.'

Peter Zonneveld was not to be put off, and set off in chase of his scoop story.

Beatrix's main concern was that The Salvation Army would now be in trouble, especially as there had been initial anxiety over the whole idea. Bosshardt was more anxious about what it all might mean to the Palace. They discussed what they should now do. Bosshardt suggested going to the Nicholas Kroese club, but Beatrix said, 'No. If they catch us indoors, they will take pictures that can be used for advertising purposes.'

As the Princess and Bosshardt walked down the Reguliersdwarsstraat, the pursuing photographers found them. As they stopped at de Lange's shoe shop, there was a flash. A photograph had been taken. A little further on and another one was taken, face on, outside the cigarette shop in the flower market. 'Is this necessary?' Bosshardt asked Zonneveld. 'Each to his job,' said Peter. 'You sell *War Crys*. I take pictures.' It was difficult to answer that.

Bosshardt and Princess Beatrix just did not know what to do. 'We'll take a taxi,' said Bosshardt. 'They haven't a car.' They stopped a taxi and jumped in; as it happened, because of a passing car, unobserved by their pursuers.

Zonneveld and his friend were mystified as to where their quarry had gone, and had to assume they had gone into the nearby hospital. They waited there for a long time!

In the taxi, Bosshardt and Princess Beatrix counted the cash they had in their pockets. It totalled five and a half guilders. 'You can drive us around as far as four and a half guilders, and we will give you a guilder tip,' said Bosshardt. 'Where do you want to go?' asked the driver. 'It doesn't matter,' said Bosshardt. 'We are being chased by two men.' 'You are not afraid, Major, are you?' asked the driver, believing such a thing to be impossible. 'No,' said Bosshardt, 'but I have a lady with me who is new to the job, and she was a bit scared by them. So we want to get rid of these men!'

The driver dropped them at Kromboomssloat, where the man lived who drove the Centre's van. They went upstairs – it was now about eleven thirty p.m. – and entered his room. 'I have brought you Princess Beatrix,' said Bosshardt.

With this family stayed a sixteen-year-old girl. Bosshardt had placed her in a private family for her own good. She told her life-story to the Princess as others had done that night. The driver said a prayer for the Princess and her family before she and Bosshardt went on to another round of smaller, quiet places, where more conversation was possible with the people of the inner city.

At one thirty a.m. Bosshardt and the Princess returned to the Goodwill Centre to find the photographers waiting on the Canal Bridge just by the Centre. They asked if they could come in, but Bosshardt replied, jocularly, that she didn't receive men at her house at such an hour. They made no comment about the Princess but asked Bosshardt: 'Major, is the woman with you looking for shelter for the night? We'll gladly help with that if she does need a place.' 'Oh, no,' said Bosshardt, 'I have plenty of room if she needs it. But she may be going home later.'

Once inside, it was time for coffee again in Bosshardt's room. At four a.m. Beatrix went home, after what she called 'the most fascinating experience of my life'.

Next day the picture of the Princess was on the front page of *De Telgraaf*. The visit and its implications took on all the facets of a seven days' wonder, but in the end all agreed a lot of *goodwill* had been created. And for the Princess, there had been the chance to meet people as they really lived.

Perhaps, too, it had its public part to play in the further evolution of Bosshardt's mission.

7

The Glory of Life

The Glory of Life is
to love, not to be loved:

to give, not get:

to serve, not to be served:

to be a strong hand in the dark
to another in time of need:

to be a cup of strength to any soul
in a crisis of weakness:

this is to know
the glory of life.

These words hang on the wall in Bosshardt's living-room-cum-office-cum-study-cum-chapel. It is the room to which Princess Beatrix was welcomed, in which she changed into her disguise, to which she returned for coffee at one thirty a.m., in which she and the Major looked at the Bible together and prayed together. It was in that same room that I received simple, generous hospitality on my stays in the Goodwill Centre. It was there she slept, thought, wrote, prayed. It was the engine room of the enormous ship captained by the Major.

To that I shall return in the next chapter. Meanwhile, it is worth looking at the meaning of being a Salvationist, for The Salvation Army is a world movement with a strong international sense and an ethos going right back to its founder, William Booth.

The first use of the term 'Salvation Army' was in 1878 although the Rev. William Booth began his work in East London much earlier – in 1865. There he founded The Christian Revival Association which subsequently became The Christian Mission. It was in May 1878 in a small appeal folder that the name The Christian Mission became The Salvation Army. Booth soon became known as its General. In August of that year a new deed poll was executed establishing the doctrines and principles of The Salvation Army. Orders and regulations for The Salvation Army were issued in October and during that year, brass instruments were first used. *War Cry* began in 1879, the year that the first cadets were trained, the first corps band was formed and the first Scottish corps was established. In 1880 the first contingent of Salvation Army officers landed in the U.S.A., while the work extended to Ireland and Australia. In 1881 it reached France, in 1882 Canada, India, Sweden and Switzerland, in 1883 Ceylon (now Sri Lanka), South Africa, New Zealand, and Pakistan, in 1884 St. Helena, in 1886 Newfoundland and Germany, and in 1887 Italy, Denmark, Jamaica. And, on May 8th in that year, the Netherlands.

The beginning of the work in the Netherlands resulted from the initiative of an English sailor named Tyler who sailed between Harwich and the Hook of Holland. He was converted and became a Salvation Army officer. Helped by a young Dutch teacher (Gerrit Govaars), he introduced the Army's work into the Netherlands. The first centre was in Amsterdam. The work soon spread throughout Holland, and in 1894 to Indonesia (then known as the Dutch East Indies). There were further advances in 1926 in Surinam and in 1927 in Curacao. Netherlands officers now serve in many areas of the world. In Holland, The Salvation Army is known as *Het Leger des Heils*, while *War Cry*, known as *Strijdkreet*, sells over one and a half million copies (1974).

The Army works in over eighty countries, uses over a hundred languages, has over sixteen thousand Corps and Outposts, has around twenty-five thousand officers plus one thousand five hundred cadets, employs a full-time un-ranked staff of over thirty-seven thousand, has over forty thousand Senior Bandsmen and over sixty-five thousand Senior Songsters and publishes over one hundred periodicals with a combined circulation of more than one million seven hundred thousand. Its social service is on a massive scale – food Distribution Centres (over two hundred serving two and a half million people), Hostels for the Homeless (nearly ten million beds are supplied in a year), prison visiting, Alcoholics' Homes, Harbour Light Centres, Homes for Women, Maternity Homes, Remand Homes and Approved Schools, Training Farms, Colonies for the Destitute, Eventide Homes, Day Nurseries, Play Centres, Seamen's and Servicemen's facilities, Night-patrol, Rescue and Anti-suicide services, Missing Persons Bureaux, Convalescent Homes, hospitals, clinics, schools, institutes, Rest Homes, etc., etc. The social work includes around one hundred and twenty Goodwill Centres of which Bosshardt's is one. No wonder the call to active, practical service is in the very life blood of the Salvationist – the word becoming the deed. It is the natural and inevitable expression of the Gospel that stands firmly at the centre of the Salvationist's life. There is, as William Booth said, the need for soap, soup and salvation, and the Army is never the Army in truth if that last category is missing.

Without it, the social service has no context. Without it, the *primary* aim of the movement has been lost.

To catch a glimpse of all that being a Salvationist means to Bosshardt, it is worth looking at the fundamental emphases of the Army.

Salvationists are 'saved to save'. Their belief that *they* have been saved from the guilt and power of sin by the grace of God, makes them soldiers committed to win others 'for Jesus Christ'. There is therefore a deliberately aggressive approach in their work, the exuberant selling of *War Cry* in public houses and from door to door, dealing personally with the unconverted, visiting people in homes or wherever they are to be found, and praying with them.

In order to make contact with the crowds who will never come inside a church or chapel, they have specialised in open-air meetings and marches during which flags, brass bands and religious songs set to 'secular' tunes are used freely.

Salvation Army *soldiers* undertake their mission voluntarily in their spare time. Officers, who are trained, devote their whole life to the service of the Army, receiving only a modest allowance to meet personal needs.

The Salvation Army has always been strict in its rules. Total abstinence for Salvationists is a commitment as is the non-smoking rule.

It has always been The Salvation Army's belief that children can begin to serve and love God, and it has geared an essential part of its work to providing interest and activities for them and for young people. One of the delights for the outsider is the sight of young people in the Army bands. Woman's place in the Army structure has always been far ahead of Women's Lib propaganda. Equal opportunity for service has always applied, even in eastern lands where the principle was not much in evidence generally.

It is worth recording the Army's message expressed first by William Booth and then by Catherine Booth:

> No resolution, religious ceremonials or pious feelings can make men good, men are in bondage to their sins ... There is no hope for permanent amendment in man without a change of heart. God is the author of this change. The greatest sinners can be changed from the power of sinful habits ...
>
> The Salvation Army's message includes the call to holiness ... a heart renewed by the Holy Ghost – put right with God, then kept right! A heart perfect in its loyalty to God, irrespective of consequences; perfect in obedience.

Movements that develop on a world scale inevitably have to adapt to local cultural situations and to express their principles, structures and outreach in ways understandable and relevant to the people they seek to serve. In doing this they may adjust and adapt to an extent that produces quite major differences of approach. We shall have to look at this point more closely as we try to appreciate the particular approach Bosshardt has brought to her unusual and indeed unique 'parish'. That said, The Salvation Army probably adapts and adjusts much less than most organisations involved in the process. Its doctrines remain defined and definite. Its rules and regulations are not changed when translated into another language. Its methods are universal. Its origin as a movement is in one man, William Booth, and even more in One behind him who is 'the same yesterday, today and forever'.

When I walked by the canals, behind the flag, the

uniforms, and the accordion on that first night in Amsterdam, I could be in the company of none other than Salvationists.

Alida Bosshardt, brilliant individualist that she is, is, as I have said, a Salvationist through and through and can be no other. The line runs down the years from its source in William Booth and across the North Sea directly to her. In the exposition of her work, her attitude, her approach, her thinking, her philosophy, we shall perhaps find unexpected slants and very personal reactions. But we shall never find other than one of those whom Bramwell Booth called 'servants of all', one who was 'saved to save'.

8

A Top-to-Toe Salvationist

THE BOSSHARDT I have presented so far is clearly no eccentric cast on the stage of life as God's fool. She would willingly be a fool for Christ's sake, if it were demanded of her. But an eccentric, no. She is an individualist who could never be contained within a rigid and confined structure – and all credit to the Army for recognising her need to be free and trusted. She is an extrovert who can walk into any situation in life, take the centre of the stage and use it for God's glory. She is a very Dutch lady who understands her people – at every level. She can confer with authority and commune with prostitutes. She is the guardian of a life-style that is authentically Christian – simple, disciplined, dedicated, devout. She is a humorist who can laugh at herself and her situation, but who knows how to shed tears of pain over others' problems. She is courageous to a degree and generous to a fault. And all of these things, wedded to the chance factors in life – someone's decision to do a 'This is Your Life' about her, for example – have made her a public figure of great stature, the friend of royalty and high officialdom, the representative to modern Dutch society of the Christian faith in action.

All this she has had to carry without a background of extended academic studies, or of vast specialist training – though she did, just for this reason, take the social work diploma I have referred to. As with Topsy in Uncle Tom's Cabin, her work has 'just growed', and the responsibilities of that growth have grown ever bigger.

For that reason, Bosshardt, for many years, has been

invited to give lectures, public addresses, radio programmes, etc., on her work, a process which has compelled her to reflect on the things she has had to do and the reasons for her continuing involvement in the work. Within that context, however nonconformist in her attitudes to her work and however untraditional her methods of ministry, she has always spoken as a Salvationist.

It is for this reason that I return to the image of ‘the Major’ (as she has become known nationally) as captain of an enormous ship. For it is only through that image that it is possible to see the breadth, variety, diversity and depth of her work yet feel, at the same time, how much she is in control of the operation. And being in control means operating wholly from her Salvationist base, whatever the individuality she displays in one large sector of her outreach.

There are many who associate Bosshardt’s work *solely* with the Red Light area and all that that emotive phrase implies, and there are some who criticise her on the basis of her approach to that work, for that approach is, for them, controversial. Critics however seem to forget that Bosshardt’s work is far, far wider than the Red Light ministry. She is in charge of *all* ‘Goodwill Work’ in the Netherlands and in direct control of it in her own area in central Amsterdam. But, in Army terms, you cannot possibly have social work, or ‘Goodwill Work’ in the Netherlands and in direct control Gospel. This has been repeated and emphasised, both by Colonel Bosshardt and by others in high places in the Army in the Netherlands. If the Government (as it may well do, in the future) gives subsidy to social work only if it is divorced from evangelical work, the Army would refuse the subsidy. It is not a secular, social work organisation. It is a Christian organisation engaged in outreach for Christian reasons, and 'goodwill work' is the point at which contact is made with the world, where no other point of contact exists.

Bosshardt spoke vehemently on this when I met her. 'If the State tells us we must only do social work from nine to five, and we must act like other social work agencies, or we won't get financial support, I will say, "Stop our money and we will find it ourselves." We do not function from nine to five. Human problems do not end at five o'clock. They are there twenty-four hours a day, so we are needed twenty-four hours a day.' And she herself has put that into practice all her life. 'It is not human to stop being concerned when the office shuts. That may be all right for professional social work, but not for The Salvation Army.'

Bosshardt, as a social worker, has professional skills to offer within her ministry, and this she does, but never once has she lost the sense of balance that puts 'the spiritual' first. She is Salvationist always, social worker when necessary.

The Salvationist role and the social worker role come together in ministry to the girls. There the *method* becomes important and must be understood. But no one can know Bosshardt personally and suggest that, in some way, she is in danger of leaving the Salvationist part of her behind her when the acceptance and involvement of the social worker come into play. It is simply not true. It never has been true and it never will be true.

> And now, hallelujah! the rest of my days
> Shall gladly be spent in promoting His praise
> Who opened His bosom to pour out this sea
> Of boundless salvation for you and for me.

Listen to Bosshardt quoting these words and you know she is giving her credo, at any and every point in her life. 'What is the life of holiness but the endeavour, as God shall give us grace, to translate the Gospel we preach into a pattern of daily living?' wrote General Frederick Coutts when head of the Army. This is Bosshardt incarnate. Can there be anyone who more fulfils all that statement offers than Bosshardt? I doubt it.

It is imperative then, if one is going to see her specialist work in perspective, to appreciate the breadth and depth of her total involvement. She is corps officer, then social worker. 'I am never out on social work on Sunday at a time when there is worship going on. I am either leading it or involved in worship somewhere else. But worship is the first priority.' Her ministry embraces all that is involved in 'spiritual work' – running the corps and 'social work' – running the Goodwill Centre. 'I believe,' she says, 'that the combination of a personal experienced religion and a good education in the social sciences have put a mark on the work,' They have, but it is the former which is the ship's engine-room.

Bosshardt talks excitedly and authoritatively on this basic question of the relationship between what she calls evangelism and social assistance. She will deny that the question is 'social work and its relationship to pastoral care'. 'It is the reverse,' she says. 'The Salvation Army is primarily an evangelical movement, but I have never felt that the purpose and methods of evangelisation and social aid are in conflict. They aren't. In any case, the client knows when approaching The Salvation Army what it stands for. Man is a religious and a socially-minded creature. He finds the combination of these needs are met in the Army. The Salvationist is expected to be dually professional in evangelism *and* social work.'

What is it then that makes some people cautious, if not critical, of Bosshardt's work in the Red Light context? Certainly unfamiliarity with her in her basic

Salvationist role. 'I'm a Salvation Army soldier from top to toe' runs an old chorus, and Mrs. Commissioner Mona Westergaard, quoting that in relation to the Bosshardt she knows so well adds: 'She *thinks* Army, *talks* Army, *projects* the Army, *safeguards* the Army, privately, publicly . . .'

But the main anxiety of her critics must go deeper. It has to do with the way in which she works out acceptance of the Red Light situation. No one would easily talk as she does to the prostitutes: 'Only one client tonight? That's terrible. You should give it up,' she will say. Or 'How is business? Aren't you tired of it? Why not shut the shop?' The significance and importance in Christian terms of an 'accepting' attitude I shall deal with at length later, for it is so relevant to all mission, evangelism and pastoral care today. Here I only comment that, as with every area and subject in life, quoting sentences out of context is dangerous and unfair. Until you meet, hear and walk with Bosshardt, and correctly interpret the tone and aim of the comments made in her characteristically husky voice, it is very unwise to generalise.

Perhaps most deeply felt by some is the fear that her attitude of acceptance in the Red Light situation involves a failure to do what The Salvation Army would want to do – condemn the whole trade in sex and lust out of hand and have nothing to do with it at all. Keeping distance from evil and avoiding contact with it would be the better part. But such an attitude does not at all reflect the demands of One who was 'Friend of publicans, and sinners' and who descended into hell and 'took on' the might of evil at its worst. Nor has it ever seemed to be the way of the Army. For the Army has, beyond all others, been able to mix with and lift up the dregs of humanity in Christ's name. Of course Bosshardt condemns the practitioners of perversion, the dealers in drugs, the profiteers in prostitution. Of course, she sees it all as a way of life contrary to God's purpose. Of course, she is not condoning sin. 'It is the sinner I am concerned about. How, or where, can we meet her (or him) in the time of need, if we are not there in the midst?' How that 'being there' is worked out, I shall tell, shortly. It is enough to say now that ministering to the alcoholic in his self-inflicted stupor is no validation of drink; ministering to a distressed and distraught girl after an abortion says nothing commendatory about abortion itself. 'I have to hate the sin, but love the sinner,' says Bosshardt. 'How can I do it if I am not there?'

So Bosshardt talks of the difference in purpose and methods of pastoral care (evangelism and care) and the giving of social aid (which includes 'social work' from a technical point of view). 'The purpose and methods of evangelical and pastoral care are of a different nature,' she says. 'The former is geared to supernatural truths and the latter to life in the world today and man's ability to adapt to it. But it all has to do with humanity, so an integration of the two methods should be possible. They have much in common. Within evangelism, we use numerous principles borrowed from social casework, for example.'

Bosshardt, in talking about these two areas, constantly comes back to the theme of 'broken contact'. She sees so much trouble caused by loss of contact with God. 'In evangelism and pastoral care, we try to speak of the broken contact between God and man and the need for reconciliation.' So evangelism involves the ministry of the Word, the offering of the Gospel to *all wherever they are and however far off the awful country to which they have gone*, 'with the purpose of bringing them to the Faith.' Pastoral care for Bosshardt is 'the work of the Shepherd bringing comfort and guidance through the Word in order to build up faith and deepen spiritual lives.' So Bosshardt says, with conviction and emphasis: 'The purpose of both evangelism and pastoral care is the preaching of the Word that is not of ourselves but is of God; the Word of forgiveness, renewal and hope, revealed in and through Christ.' 'It is always like this,' she says with emphasis:

Christ for the world,
The world for Christ.

'This Word, from God through Christ, brings restoration of the broken contact between God and man, which took place with man's fall from grace. To bring about his restoration is the task of all involved in pastoral care.'

I have listened to Bosshardt talk and I have heard her preach in a crowded hospital church – in the Andreaskapel at the Andreas Ziekenhuis. This woman speaks from the very centre of the faith as understood by Salvationists. She is *in* a world *of* which she is not. She is totally disciplined on moral issues important to the Army, so, for example, there is no place for alcohol or smoking in her life. She is in touch with the deep things of the Spirit and can bring these deep things into situations with which none of us could easily cope – an impromptu prayer at the bar in a club bringing silence to a motley throng intent on sensual enjoyment. She is *never* out of the uniform that stands for enrolment as a soldier in the army of the Lord.

Let Bosshardt say it for herself:

I was asked to take part in a festivity in one of the more distinctive houses in one of the suburbs of Amsterdam. A lady was celebrating her fortieth birthday. She was divorced a long time previously and now was living with a very young friend of twenty-five years of age and her own son of fifteen. For many years she had been employed in prostitution but, in her own opinion, she had made an improvement by no longer exercising this profession personally, but by running some houses where young girls were working for her.

They had made quite a feast for her birthday. People from all kinds of backgrounds were present. I was there together with a colleague social worker – not a Salvationist. After having spoken for half an hour with one and another and having felt out the atmosphere, I asked for a moment's silence from the festival noise, music, dance and drinking. With the aid and under the guidance of the Lord, I then had the privilege of testifying about the God who says through the prophet Nahum (1:15): 'O Judah, keep thy solemn feasts, perform thy vows.' Many of those present at the feast knew something about God and His Salvation through our Saviour Jesus Christ and possibly also something about the Holy Spirit who makes us conscious of these things. I spoke to them for a few minutes and I testified about my personal spiritual life and the power that everybody can find in faith in God. I then prayed for them and especially for 'Dolly', the guest of the feast, for her son, for her friend and for all of us there.

Yes, indeed, a top-to-toe Salvationist.

9

Sitting Where They Sit

THE MAGAZINE *OUI* is not one I would have expected to find in Bosshardt's living-room. It lived, I felt, uneasily with the main thrust of the literature on her bookshelves – *The Essentials of Christian Experience* by General Coutts, *God in the Shadows* by Hugh Redwood, *Born to Battle* by Sallie Chesham, *The General next to God* by Richard Collier, and so on. Yet Bosshardt handed it (or more exactly four pages torn from it) to me with what seemed to be pride and pleasure. I wondered why.

OUI is (to judge by the four pages) another in that proliferation of pornographic or semi-pornographic publications that have presented the results of the sexual revolution in pictorial splendour and claimed they are doing a service to mankind in the liberation they represent. Their contribution to that which is 'good and lovely and of good report' is not obvious, although they claim to be artistic and would be offended if called coarse and vulgar. That there is a vast public for such periodicals is simply fact. The enormous success (in commercial terms) of *Penthouse*, *Playboy* and a whole succession of competitors is ample evidence of the popularity of literature of this kind.

One of the features of these magazines is often the inclusion of serious and important material of quality. One of the best articles ever written on nuclear war appeared in an edition of *Playboy*, I am told, and certainly contributors to these journals have included names drawn surprisingly from ecclesiastical circles!

OUI, it would appear, follows that pattern. I would

not on the whole have expected Bosshardt's platform for comment on the problems and perils of prostitution to be *OUI*, but it was. And I think she felt a degree of satisfaction that it was so.

Perhaps that rather (at first sight) surprising relationship of Bosshardt and *OUI* says something that is important and fundamental to her point of view. To use a concept already mentioned, she is wholly *in* this world of prostitution, but is not *of* it. This is important. It certainly has a familiar ring in terms of our Lord's attitude to this world generally. His disciples must be *in* this world, but they are never *of* it. Bosshardt has taken that seriously.

The article as a whole is a ghastly survey of the modern Sodom and Gomorrha (or so it feels) presented as the attractions of modern Amsterdam. To prove the point would involve producing quotations that degrade and disgust, so the evidence must be taken as read. It far outweighs the catalogue of sins against which St. Paul inveighs early in Romans. But the middle section switches to quotations from a conversation with Bosshardt. These deal with her views on the 'liberated prostitute'.

'There is no such thing as bad publicity. There is only publicity.' So the accepted rule runs in the public relations business, and those who are used to the attitudes of professionals in that field will not argue too long over the maxim. Bosshardt is an expert operator in the field of free publicity as well as (as we have already seen) one with an eye for a chance. She took it with the bishop who filled her collecting box, instead of persuading her to change her decision to join the Army. She seized it the moment she recovered from the shock of finding herself the subject of 'This is Your Life' and bought and furnished a centre as a result. If you can throw a word in for Christ, or The Salvation Army, in the midst of un-Christian things, something good has been done. Perhaps even the opportunity to say a word *for* and on behalf of the girls – her parishioners, her people, her friends – made it all worthwhile.

Perhaps her sense of oneness with those girls is witnessed to in her own dramatic self-description as a 'kind of Christian call-girl', a brave declaration, but not one of bravado. She is 'in', but not 'of'. Her pride and pleasure, I suspected, lay in having got into the literature of the sensual world a word on behalf of the Word of God.

Bosshardt's ministry in the inner city has been (to quote Ezekiel) to 'sit where they sit', to live *in* a work situation *of* which she can never be part, and so to accept the realities of that world and exercise ministry in relation to those realities. It is for that reason that she can do what many from backgrounds similar to mine, find it very hard to do – to accept the prostitute and her trade *as a profession*. The profession accepted as a reality, its rules must be respected. The prostitute has her place of work, very often her employers, and all the occupational hazards of her profession. The act of intercourse is the supreme expression of human love, the ultimate communion between two people in love, and it is 'wrong' and 'sinful' when it is taken out of that context and made a physical act of human satisfaction unrelated to a deep and loving relationship. Christians, like many others, would see it in that context. Others, able to accept the act of intercourse as something possible with more than one person and even with many as a legitimate part of sexual maturity, would still relate that act to love, affection, emotion, sincerity, etc. And there are many who would violently deny this way of life to be promiscuous. Others still would set a lesser value on intercourse and see it as no more than the modern equivalent of a good-night kiss, something to be expected in the 'liberated' atmosphere of today. But it would still involve some feeling, however temporary, however slight. It is not easy to empathise with this last attitude, but it is there in contemporary society, for better or worse.

For the prostitute, none of these prescribed and possible relationships apply; not even the last. Prostitution is a job. There may be times when the job of work is more enjoyable, more satisfying and more fulfilling, as most find in their professional work, but in the end it is no more and no less than a job of work to be done professionally and efficiently, for the client who is there to pay for it. So Bosshardt says in *OUI*: 'The girls aren't victims of sinister social forces. They do it for money. Then they retire and get a candy shop or something. Sure, most of them support a man, but this man is their boyfriend. The clients are business. The boyfriend is an emotional relationship.'

It is this fundamental acceptance by her of the trade as a reality, that establishes Bosshardt's acceptance by those within it. The presence of the Army uniform is not seen as that of the do-gooder who comes to interfere, to ban, to criticise, to challenge the trade. The challenge is implicitly there (the challenging part of comfort) for no one confronted by the good, the Christ (and that uniform always brings Christ into the picture), can fail to be conscious of the contrast between life as it is lived and life as it might be. But the battle is not on that front. Bosshardt is not there to condemn, only to save, and the 'saving' is not going to be effected realistically by constant harangue against the only way prostitutes believe they can earn their living.

The fact that Bosshardt knows by name some two-thirds of the three thousand or so girls in the area means relationships with them are real in some sense. The others she will know by sight as part of the district. The new ones she will come to know, for perhaps it is at the point of entry to the profession that the hope lies of making a lasting impact.

The justification of Bosshardt's approach and her understanding of the facts of their lives is constantly borne out by events. When an evangelical group moved in to condemn the 'sin and evil' that was going on all around, the end result was violence and one of their number thrown into a canal. There is no violence against Bosshardt – the whole community and no doubt its toughest characters would rise up in vengeance to protect their Major if anyone attacked *her*. The capacity to be a friend of publicans and sinners creates its own response. The publicans and sinners will rise up in wrath when their real friend is touched.

As I have hinted, it may not be easy for all who read this book to feel that Bosshardt's approach to ministry in this situation is 'right'. And this is understandable. There is that strong and real biblical strain to which I have referred that counsels avoidance of contact with evil in any form, that fears such contact may bring corruption in its wake, that believes that public condemnation of manifest sin and evil is the Christian duty and responsibility. And of course it is. Any form of life that reduces the quality of life for mankind is subject material for the modern prophet who fails in his or her responsibility if evil wherever seen is not denounced. The danger of judgment especially of a moral kind, however, is failure to apply the judgment to oneself. The prophet is not himself or herself necessarily the perfect person – for if this be the qualification, no prophet shall there ever be. The prophetic function is that of interpreting the forces behind and underneath events and having done so, demonstrating where life is going and what catastrophe will come if things are not changed. In doing that, the prophet speaks not on his own authority, but on one outside himself. So judgment of this kind must be made. But it is still necessary, as the first apostles were reminded, to be 'wise as serpents' in the work of the Kingdom. The peripatetic prophet who moves into the Red Light area for a moment to hurl his verbal rocks at the manifest evil that he sees has no hope ofsreal effect. The only real hope lies in constant witness in word and deed by those who sit where they sit, who are in the world and understand it, yet are not of it.

It is in this way that Bosshardt's mission has taken on aspects of the miraculous. It is also an extraordinary comment on its consistency that the miracle has worked for over thirty years. Think of it – thirty years! Where were *you* thirty years ago? What have *you* been doing since then and all the time between? Could you begin to think of coping, night and day, year in, year out, with trouble and pain, sin and the sordid, crisis and disaster, tragedy and tumult, with ministry like this?

There are fundamentally two possible attitudes, not mutually exclusive, to 'the world' and its situations. One is to seek to challenge them and change them. The other is to seek to minister to people within those situations, to comfort them and to care. Both these functions are necessary. The former was especially associated with the prophets who declared wrong structures, policies and people to be opposition to God and in His name called for change. The latter is the responsibility accepted by all who feel called to a caring role whether priest, counsellor, social worker, pastor, psychotherapist or whatever. These roles are, I repeat, not mutually exclusive. One of the automatic results of 'comforting' can be challenge to an existing way of life. But there is enough distinction between them to allow their representing these different facets of reaction to any situation.

It is so clear that it goes without saying that, from a Christian point of view, to challenge and therefore to try to get rid of the whole paraphernalia of prostitution, pornography and all the degraded commercialism that goes with it would be a blessing to humanity. Even those who take the most permissive of contemporary viewpoints and argue (as the Dutch seem to do) that as sensual humanity exists as a fact, it is better to confine it to a corner, could never defend the appalling degradation this reaches in some aspects of the life of modern Amsterdam.

But Bosshardt is a realist. There is not the slightest possibility on earth that any influence she has or could create could lead to the closing down of the Red Light area, and that she accepts. Her call is to minister in Christ's name *within* that factual situation and it is this she has set out to do and which she does to the utmost of her ability. So the energy that would be wasted on the hopeless task of challenging all the financial, political and social vested interests in maintaining the Red Light area is better channelled into the comforting ministry of Christ's servants to those who are there for better or for worse, for richer or for poorer, in sickness and in health. It may be that for an individual here, a family there, the ministry of comfort will bring its own challenge and pressure to change a way of life (how often has Bosshardt seen that happen), but the emphasis is on the kind of comforting that is relevant ministry in a situation that is unlikely to be changed fundamentally and has not in fact been changed for the better for many years.

'Evangelism sets standards,' Bosshardt told me, 'but it "accepts" also. Social work has as its starting-point acceptance, but it also sets standards.'

You do not cease to be the prophet of God by 'sitting where they sit'. He did not cease to be the Saviour of the world by descending into hell. Bosshardt is not less, but more a Salvationist, in living among and ministering to publicans and sinners.

Here is my hand!

The Glory of Life is to . . .

I sat where they sat . . .

We are saved . . . to save

Neither do I condemn thee . . .

The Friend of publicans and sinners

God gave His Son not to condemn the world,
but that the world might be saved . . .

This is the Lord's doing
Is it not marvellous . . . miraculous?

10

Love Incarnate . . .

Love came down at Christmas,
Love incarnate, Love divine . . .

I HAVE SET down some of Bosshardt's theories of evangelism, pastoral care and social aid, but whatever she is, she is no mere academic theorist, offering doctrinaire solutions to hypothetical situations. If anyone is a 'doer of the Word', it is Bosshardt. She is pragmatic to a degree, and cannot find herself in any situation without getting involved. Wherever she is, her reaction is always to *do* something and do it at once.

There was, for example, one occasion when, in the early hours of the morning, she met one of the girls struggling along one of the cobbled streets of the district. She was limping badly, almost wholly unable to walk because of sore feet caused by shoes with very high heels in the contemporary manner. Seeing the Salvation Army bonnets of Bosshardt and a colleague, she automatically sought help from them. 'Of course you can borrow my shoes if you want to,' said Bosshardt, 'but you'll have to come with me to the Goodwill Centre to get them, for I am certainly not going to wear yours!' The prostitute went back to her lodgings wearing Bosshardt's shoes. 'You have seen the last of them' said a visitor who happened to be at the Centre. But she was wrong. The shoes were returned, none the worse for being borrowed. It surprised the visitor, but of course not Bosshardt, who had never even been conscious of the possibility that they would not be returned. The relationship built up between her and 'the girls' over twenty years is quite special, and implies, strange as it may seem, a *mutual* respect and trust.

I asked Bosshardt about many of the situations she met and dealt with in terms of her philosophy of caring. Let her tell some stories of 'Love incarnate'.

There was for example, Tiny.

Bosshardt got to know Tiny when she was nineteen years old. She was the youngest child in a family of seven children and came from a small provincial town in the east of the country. She was a difficult girl, perhaps because her parents were really too old to be able to cope with a young, growing girl of this kind.

Between fourteen and eighteen, the situation at home grew steadily worse, so she ran away from home. She had no sense of belonging there and, though she had many casual boyfriends, she made no real relationships.

Tiny wanted to be in the city, so she came to Amsterdam and found a job in domestic service. This was not a success and within the following six months she had three jobs and found herself out of work. She then got to know a nice but very weak young man who made her pregnant, so she had to marry.

The young man had a very strong attachment to his mother while Tiny sought amusement in pubs and cafés of less repute, in spite of being married and having a child. She tried to solve the problem of her loneliness in casual relationships.

From pub-frequenter to bar-hostess was one short step and, within the first six months of her marriage, she had become a street-walker. The marriage still existed, but *he* stayed at home while *she* earned their living. Her mother-in-law, who was sorry for the plight of her son, cared for the baby.

However hard we tried to make real contact with Tiny, says Bosshardt, in order to offer her serious social aid, it was impossible to do so, although a superficial contact was established. 'She would not accept the advice or counsel which I felt was the real task in regard to her marriage and family responsibilities.' She became more and more deeply involved in prostitution.

Her mother-in-law died, so her husband went to the Council for Child Protection with the child as he alone could not care for the child.

A divorce followed, and the child was handed over to the Child Welfare service, followed by the withdrawal of custody from both parents. It was placed in the care of a foster parents' institute and, when suitable parents were found in the south of Holland, the child was sent there.

Bosshardt maintained contact with Tiny who had now become one of the 'window' prostitutes. She visited her regularly and found, strangely enough, that the point of contact in Tiny's case was always the Gospel. Says Bosshardt:

> She often stood and listened when we held our open-air meetings and now and then attended our meetings, sometimes under the influence of drink. Now and again she would ask for a *War Cry*, or she would come and ask if she could telephone her sister. She told us that her family background was a religious one, that she used to attend the Reformed Church regularly and that she had once belonged to the church club for girls. Now that she was older and began to look back over her life, she remembered all these things.

Bosshardt goes on:

We tried to be tolerant and understanding, and to meet her on this religious ground, going just as far as she was ready to go at that time. Gradually we saw her more frequently at the meetings and she asked for counselling. Then she would disappear for weeks, only to turn up once more and we would start again from the beginning.

When I visited her, I was able to speak to her not only about her difficulty in adjusting to society (she could not accept the normal behavioural pattern of a woman) but also to refer to her spiritual needs, which drove her to seek help in worship. This combination of evangelical approach and social case work led, in the end, to her leaving prostitution. Later she married a transport driver and found a new life. As they say of her in our district, 'She is going straight now. She has been converted.' In other words she has come to a personal, spiritual knowledge of God. Conversion meant, in her case, a miraculous strengthening of her will-power, and she is now a good soldier of The Salvation Army.

Tiny is often reminded of the past and naturally she longs to be reunited with her child who is now cared for by foster-parents, and whose whereabouts are unknown to her. Bosshardt adds: 'The methods of social work must be maintained however, and we have to make it clear to her that a seven-year-old child cannot be uprooted. I have visited the foster-parents who have now formally adopted the child and seen that he is happy there, that the bonds are strong and healthy between child and foster-parents, and that it is better that things remain as they are, at least for the time being. Tiny has to learn to accept the consequences of her former life, to feel secure in her present situation and to build a worthwhile future based on her faith.

It is a moving and impressive example of a combination of spiritual and social help.

It is a good example of Love Incarnate.

Sonja grew up in a family with a step-father. She was the illegitimate child of her mother and another man, born before her marriage to Sonja's step-father. Neither she nor her mother had any further contact with her natural father. Bosshardt says she got to know Sonja when she was fifteen years old, and in the hands of the Amsterdam juvenile police. None of the probation societies would accept responsibility for her because she was completely unmanageable. The juvenile psychiatrist at the city health service had given up all hope for her future.

Sonja was thought to be pregnant. She had had many boyfriends and had sexual relationships with them. She had however fallen in love with a man of thirty, a 'pimp' who had eventually introduced her to prostitution. Because she was under age and not married, the juvenile police stepped in, but she behaved so badly in the various homes to which she was sent that she was quickly thrown out of them. She announced that she was going to get married, but at the very door of the city hall, she changed her mind and refused to go through with the ceremony. The same day she was back 'in business' but soon found herself in the juvenile prison again.

Let Bosshardt tell the story:

> Sonja was completely indifferent and unco-operative. Her friend was imprisoned in another part of the country for his part in the affair. All this took

place in the month of November. In December, we heard her story and went to visit her. We requested the authorities to allow Sonja to enter our new house for such cases (it was now obvious that a baby was expected) and before Christmas she came to the Ruytenburgh, which has accommodation for about ten women or girls who have, in some way or other, been involved in prostitution. But Sonja was very much out of place, as she was so much younger than the others. We found a pleasant family of Salvationists in the district (simple people, father, mother and two boys) and Sonja was welcome there. First there was a visit to the hairdresser, some nice new clothes, and off she went. The homely and pleasant mother created the right atmosphere and soon she was accepted, with her own place in the family.

The results were satisfactory. Sonja started to attend the meetings with the family and was influenced spiritually. She was accepted for herself both in terms of her religious experience and also in relation to her social work contacts. The baby was born in June and, at her request, the child was dedicated to God. She and the child still have their place in the family that so warmly received her. She herself has a job and, after work, she looks after her daughter, Vera, herself.

Sonja's redemption and rehabilitation is the result of spiritual and social work in combination.

She is also the result of Love Incarnate.

Annie grew up in a Christian home. Her parents had serious marriage problems, but because of their strict religious views and because of their children, a divorce was out of the question.

Annie had one older sister and two younger brothers. The brothers, after secondary school, attended university, one reading medicine and the other law. The older sister was not so successful at school. She returned home, but because of her inability to settle caused all kinds of trouble.

Annie, having completed secondary school, started medical studies, switching later to psychology. After a year she started to drink heavily, became involved in student social life, seeking continual new sexual relationships and so was gradually dragged down into prostitution. Then she stopped drinking. She was now twenty-one, an intelligent young woman but, having found herself a flat in the heart of Amsterdam, she furnished it tastefully and set herself up as a prostitute.

Bosshardt takes up the story:

> I met her on my rounds. She herself told me her story. As Salvationist-social worker, I visit her weekly with the *War Cry* and she reads it regularly. Sometimes she has a visitor when I call. Sometimes she has gone to the theatre with friends, or to a film or a concert. Sometimes she is having driving lessons. She has regular holidays too.
>
> I have been visiting her regularly now for four years, showing interest in her, accepting her as she is. In shorter or longer conversations, I have spoken to her occasionally about spiritual things. There were also our social contacts, the offer of clothing for the small son of her charwoman, a week's holiday for the son of her landlady, a ticket for the midnight mass for a neighbour who was a Catholic, and a Bible for herself.
>
> She then needed help with other matters, for instance the period she went through when she

thought it would be better for her if she emigrated, but because of her being in prostitution, she was unable to obtain the necessary bill of good conduct, to enable her to be issued with a passport. After six months of visiting the authorities, the papers came through. By then she had decided not to emigrate, but the passport was a treasured possession, and useful if and when she wanted to make trips abroad. We were also able to advise her when she had persistent stomach complaints, and to persuade her to have medical attention. She was given medicine, and when she had a particularly sleepless period, she said it was due to the fact that she was still in conflict over her former religious background and her present way of life.

Here again was an opportunity for the social worker to be an evangelist. Bosshardt says:

I tried to help her, in her self-assessment, to ask herself: 'Who am I? What do I want of life and what are the possibilities I have?' Time was also on our side. She got to know a student who was reading economics and, although his parents were shocked when they knew of his friendship, they became more and more devoted to each other. In the last year and a half of his study, he moved in with her and, as his parents had withdrawn their financial support, she earned enough to pay his study and to keep them both in reasonable comfort.

The student's parents approached me several times and asked me to help get him out of Annie's clutches. But they were very happy in their small flat, had a car, and, when he had to be away on field-study, she earned their living. While he was at home they lived for each other and enjoyed the many forms of cultural life that had always interested her. He finally took his degree and they were married and bought a charming house in a small village in the province of Utrecht where he works in the city, and she is completely 'resocialised'. His parents have accepted her and nobody in the village knows of her past.

Annie proudly tells Bosshardt how happy they are now, how they regularly attend church and do so because of their own spiritual awareness and need. 'I have no more underworld friends now and my church-going neighbours have become our real friends. I am so glad to be out of the life I lived for more than seven years,' Annie says.

This is another example of the integration of spiritual and social work on the Bosshardt model, remembering that Annie 'expected a message of evangelism from the Salvationist-social worker, and accepted this message as a "plus". The methods of social case work were used in the work of evangelism. The first contacts with the woman, and also with her husband, constituted the relationship within which it is possible to offer spiritual counsel and guidance, whenever necessary.'

Is not this the Lord's doing and is it not 'marvellous in our eyes', this example of Love Incarnate?

Herman is a homosexual, aged thirty-two, a nurse in a hospital for psychiatric patients. He is a Protestant. During his military service, he had had contact with a minor and, while in the services, this became known and Herman was taken to court. He spent eight months in prison, in the Hague, and was later bound over for four months with a three-year probation period. From prison he came to Amsterdam because his parents lived there, and he moved in with his sister who had three young children.

The Salvation Army was the probationary organisation chosen by him, and, from the time he came back to Amsterdam, he continued to attend The Salvation Army meetings, where he seemed to find some measure of religious satisfaction.

Bosshardt says:

> As a social worker, I was responsible for his case and we talked about his problems. He was always conscious of the fact that he was a delinquent, and his family always remind him of this. He found work as store keeper in a large factory on the outskirts of Amsterdam and was given quite a responsible job to do. He did not stay long with his sister, as he and his brother-in-law do not see eye-to-eye and, after both his father and mother died, he was asked to find another place to live. At the death of his mother, he had asked me to officiate at the burial, and although he was the eldest son, I felt we must ask the sister first. There was no objection, and this led to a spiritual contact with the family, during which we were able to read the Scriptures together and have prayers.
>
> The social contact continued. Herman found a room with an old lady who was delighted with him. He was very tidy and clean. He scrubbed the stairs and cleaned the hall for her, took care that the kitchen was always tidied up after he or the other lodgers had used it. There were problems, however. He could not accept others who asked for rooms in the same house, and, when he gained a regular friend, relationships with the other boarders became very strained.
>
> After he had lived there for two years and the

landlady continued to be satisfied with him, his probationary period was completed and my monthly visits were no longer necessary. There are no problems now with minors. He is accepted as he is by the group of Salvationists and he takes part in the indoor and outdoor activities of the Centre.

The housing problem is, however, the biggest one. He would be very happy if he and his friend could find a house where they would not be boarders. Both are more than thirty years old. I have visited the housing authorities who are willing to listen if two women wish to share a house, but they take a different view when they know I speak on behalf of two men. Once he nearly had a flat, and on another occasion a small two-roomed house, but without the permission of the housing authorities, it was impossible to be given tenancy.

All this was very disappointing. Herman developed stomach trouble and became so ill that he had to be taken to hospital to have an ulcer operated on. After a convalescent period, he recovered fully. I have tried to help him find quietness and confidence in his faith, so that he may learn not only to accept others as they are, but to accept himself, and to have more confidence in the future.

We were at last able to find a two-roomed apartment in the city, and after a good deal of discussion, a permit was granted for Herman's tenancy.

This Bosshardt offers as yet another example of the social worker's individual approach. It includes again an acceptance of *facts*, but it is not an acceptance that makes a judgment on those facts. Comments Bosshardt: 'Herman's being accepted by the group, his development of a personal faith in God, which has also led to his strengthened will-power to overcome his particular problems, have all led to his adaptation to his situation and his effort to work through his difficulties.'

It is an example of the power of Love Incarnate.

Within the structure of the social work run from the Goodwill Centre, there are opportunities for evangelical work such as visiting cafés, etc., with a message in word and song and prayer. Bosshardt tells the story: 'One Friday night the open-air activities of the Goodwill Centre were in full swing, when, round about midnight, there was a request for us to visit the café belonging to "tante Ali", who is also the landlady of the nine girls who hire a room from her. It was her birthday.' The soldiers and officers, led by Bosshardt, sing their message, testify and pray, while everyone in the crowded café listens intensely to the Word being proclaimed.

Two of the girls, aged nineteen and twenty-one, ask Bosshardt when it might be possible for them to come and have a talk. A meeting is arranged. 'Thus two new contacts are made for the social aspect of the work,' says Bosshardt, 'through the pastoral and evangelical work we seek to carry out.'

Love came down at Christmas,
Love Incarnate . . .
Love Divine . . .

11

'Neither Do I Condemn Thee . . .'

THE STORY OF the woman taken in adultery in St. John's Gospel has, in the New English Bible, been taken out of the main text and added at the end of the Gospel. This is on the ground that manuscript evidence for its authenticity is questionable. The passage has however (to use J. B. Phillips's phrase) an extraordinary 'ring of truth' about it. It feels so authentically Jesus. Its invention by others would be extraordinary. I am not qualified to pass academic judgment on the passage. All I can testify to is that 'ring of truth'.

It is a story about judgment, but essentially the judgment one is compelled to make on oneself and not judgment imposed from outside. The woman was produced as a kind of Exhibit No. 1 by those who sought such an external, authoritative, and indeed authoritarian, judgment. Jesus puts the ball back into their own court. 'Let him who is without sin cast the first stone.' He did not need to offer judgment. They judged themselves and slipped away, 'the eldest first'. The woman was left with the inevitability of judgment from the holy one before whom she had been brought as a first-class example of the sin of adultery 'caught in the very act'. The Law said she must be stoned. Christ said, 'Neither do I condemn thee . . .'

The surprise this incident contains is reflected in the surprise some may still feel at Bosshardt's deep involvement in ministry to people who, not for one moment being just 'caught in the act', have made the act their profession. It is not Bosshardt's purpose or function to bring a judgmental attitude to these professionals. This has nothing to do with an inability to be severe. Far from it. There is, as we have seen, a toughness about Bosshardt that is real and active. There are times when people who come for sympathy are sent back to their situations and told why they must do this, in no uncertain terms. There are the club and pub owners, hard men in a hard world, with whom Bosshardt will deal without fear. There is many a mere male used to the tough life who has wilted under Bosshardt's honest words. There is all the ability to add (as Jesus did) 'go and sin no more' and mean it. There is all the background of Salvation Army doctrine implanted in and imprinted on her mind: and there is nothing grey about Salvation Army doctrine. 'We believe that ... in consequence of our first parents' fall, all men have become sinners, totally depraved, and as such are justly exposed to the wrath of God,' it says under the heading of Salvationist doctrines in the Army's official Year Book. 'We believe ... in the general judgment at the end of the world, in the eternal happiness of the righteous: and in the endless punishment of the wicked.' There is not much grey about that! But Bosshardt had learnt, in the only place she could, of the way the Gospel must be expressed in the world of which she is not. That way is the way of acceptance and ministry within acceptance.

So often Christian preaching and help has been offered to people only in relation to the position in which they ought to be. The result has been lack of empathy, understanding and relevance. The answers given bear no relationship to the questions asked, and people, far from being helped, feel the irrelevance of 'the church'. The only place that ministry can start is where people are. The locations may be unpleasant, sordid, sad, tragic, inhuman, hopeless, but it is there that they are and only from there that they can begin to travel.

This is the meaning of the Incarnation itself. God came to where we are. He *sent* His Son into the world to share our life, to sit where we sit. His name was Emmanuel – that is *God with us*. He came to accept us as we are – for it was *while we were yet sinners*' that Christ died for us. So all the Incarnation means has to be repeated, in attitude, in ministry to others.

It is this Bosshardt has learnt through the sheer reality of her situation. It involves no casting away of her own faith, her own values, her own beliefs about life. It has simply meant learning to live alongside those *in* the world who had a totally different form of life, understanding their attitude to it, respecting the rules of the trade, and bearing witness simply by her presence to the faith she herself had.

It was never a problem for Bosshardt to pray with any of 'the girls', to read the Bible with them, to have them in for a cup of tea. It has never seemed incongruous to find some of the girls at the Sunday meetings once their professional attitude and status had been accepted as a fact. It is accepted that it would be wrong to engage a girl in conversation while a possible client was waiting, for the whole of her income and livelihood depends on the clients: it becomes part of understanding and acceptance not to encourage lost trade and lost income.

It is essential to make much of this fundamental point for only if it is appreciated, can understanding of the nature of Bosshardt's ministry follow. You cannot (metaphorically) enter the room of the prostitute, and understand, if judgment still stands in the way. You cannot see the girls as human beings 'like as we are' if condemnation alone conditions our attitudes. 'The girls have the same problems as anyone else,' says Bosshardt in *OUI*. 'Maybe it's a problem of where to live, or who's to look after the baby while mother is at work, or troubles with the boyfriend or the family. Their problems are not peculiar to prostitution.' The girls are part of humanity. If the profession they have chosen is incomprehensible as a way of life to most, that inability to empathise with the job must become irrelevant, if ministry is to be effected. All the attention and care must go towards them where they are.

It is not condemnation that this ministry is about. It is salvation.

The demand that is made on anyone who descends into hell for Christ's sake is enormous. It is a twenty-four-hour test of spiritual strength and dedication. It demands a condition of inner conviction and peace that it is not easy for human beings to maintain all the time. There is a demand made on one's humanity. Bosshardt would not separate herself from normal human beings and deny the basic instincts and feelings which go to make up being human. Analysis of human behaviour (in psychological terms) can find reasons and rationalisations for what we do and are that cast doubt on motives and uses 'the unconscious' to explain its conclusions and, as it often seems, to denigrate useful and committed activity. But that test of the Gospel still stands. 'By their fruits ye shall know them.' The ramifications of an individual's unconscious are less important than the good that they do. In any case, as James asks, 'Can a good tree produce bad fruit?' What one is, is evidence of what is inside.

But this recognition of our humanity is important.

The pressure to be not simply *in* but also *of* the world in which our ministry is set is real. The temptation to seek for popularity and acceptance can afflict the most single-minded, and bring disastrous results. The attraction of empire-building can take over, dominate and, in the end, control the simplest disciple. The sins of the flesh that 'pharisee and scribe' would claim to have overcome can express themselves in attitudes to fleshly sins that are clearly projections of a failure to come to terms with lust in their own hearts – like those who brought the woman taken in adultery. And 'there, but for the grace of God' goes any one of us. To live in intimate association with evil is, at one level, to play with fire, making wholly valid the petition 'Let us not go into temptation' for it is a dangerous place to be. The demand for personal sanctification must therefore be an overriding one, especially as we grow older and areas of life not to be experienced at all shout a little louder within for satisfaction.

The other danger is an acceptance of the need to be 'unshockable' that becomes a total insensitivity to what is wrong. Our own permissive society falls victim to this more and more, as the ever deeper plumbing of the depths of the unsanctified human unconscious takes its strangle-hold on society. As I write, England's Archbishop of Canterbury, Dr. Donald Coggan, is calling yet again for attack on the evils that 'call for the sword of the Spirit' – 'dirt on the media, far too high an abortion rate, cheapening of sex, lack of reverence for life' and so on. And on other pages of the same newspaper are reports of a planned mock crucifixion as an Easter 'entertainment' for a club's clientele and, in Denmark, a pornographic production of the life of Christ. The hell Christ descended into on the second day has always been seen as a visitation to the spirits that were in darkness, but perhaps our own contemporary descent into hell is in some way associated with the forces of darkness to which St. Paul refers, which have become incarnate in our time. If this is felt to be an overstatement, then wander through Bosshardt's parish, not so much mindful of the 'oldest profession' in which much warmth and humanity exist – because the girls are just real people – but mindful of the sinister, subtle and sinful forces which operate wherever money is to be made and which have cashed in on the obsession with gratification of the flesh. The publicists will deny it, but the smell of evil is there.

It needs a faith and conviction that is profound and total to withstand the onslaughts of mass corruption. It needs the sort of all-time commitment that the Army demands of its servants – and gets. It needs the heart in touch with the divine, and the mind set on the things of the Spirit to survive physically and spiritually. It needs the penetration of the conscious and the unconscious by the integrating sanctifying power of the Spirit to maintain and develop the Christian life in face of the living presence of evil forces. It needs the inner beauty of holiness and the outer armour of God to be sensitive to the subtle thrusts of the Tempter who quotes Scripture, searches out the Achilles' heels in our lives and intensifies his attack as we make progress in the spiritual life. For did not Christ meet the subtlest and most severe thrusts of the Tempter just after his baptism and in the conscious sense of the Holy Spirit having come upon him?

It is in the combination of this personal strength, utter conviction and practical holiness along with sensitivity and the ability to accept that Bosshardt's power and influence lies. In the shifting sands of human frailty, she appears as the rock. When all men have failed and there is nowhere to go, it is to the Goodwill Centre that the path will lead, for Bosshardt will offer her hand.

The Bosshardt story is not one of social service. It is one of Christian evangelism at the deepest level.

'Christ has no hands but our hands to do His work today.'

He has the help of one who, standing within that world of evil things, is known to be saying in His Name:

Here is my hand!

12

A Place For Everything

I HAVE TRIED in the last two or three chapters to focus on the inner strength and conviction of Bosshardt and to locate her ability to be that total Army officer, committed to all it stands for, yet with the necessary independence of spirit to adapt her Christian faith and Army practice to the quite special situation in which she lives and works. As all in the Netherlands Army structure, and most beyond it, know, Bosshardt is an individual whose best service will be given where she is left alone to offer it in her own very specific way. The Army is, in some ways, not the most flexible of organisations – as certain troubles within the organisation have shown – but over Bosshardt it has shown its willingness to give her her head and be certain results ll justify it.

We turn now to the 'publicly' in *Mrs. Commissioner Westergaard's statement* (*page 77*) for Bosshardt is constantly asked to interpret her ministry to the public, as well as to her colleagues. This she did, for example, when she talked on 'present-day ministry to the prostitute' in Amsterdam several years ago.

In looking at Bosshardt's concept of her work it may be useful also to say something briefly about the phenomenon of the presence of the most blatant pornography and prostitution in a country with a rigid Dutch Calvinist background. The phenomenon is not new, however. It may have made enormous developments in its nature and expression, but it has been a part of Amsterdam's life along the inner city canals since the time of Rembrandt. It is still something of a puzzle and a confusion to those outside Holland.

Holland is a respectable, conformist country, and a religious one historically where, as Frank Huggett, in his *The Dutch Today* writes 'even the non-believers take their faith seriously.' It is a home-loving country with a tradition of domesticity, neatness, order and cleanliness that is evident in many features of its life. Though it proclaimed itself a republic after the long eighty-year war against Spain, it has lived, generally speaking happily, under its royal family; a family that has had family and domestic ups and downs, and seriously so in recent times, but has been respected and loved by the nation. Nothing Prince Bernhard may be alleged to have done could affect Queen Juliana's personal prestige and the respect in which she is held.

Holland has changed dramatically since the Second World War. Emerging from the scarring trauma of Nazi occupation, it has made extensive and fundamental alterations in its attitudes and its way of life. It began the post-war period with its cities in ruins, Rotterdam destroyed, and a large part of its land under water. Food shortage was acute. By 1950 it had lost its empire – the Dutch East Indies – so with those resources cut off, little natural wealth, little heavy industry and few minerals, its outlook was grim.

The character of the nation did not seem able or ready to meet such a changing world. Its society was rigid and in many ways old-fashioned, a strict Calvinistic morality still operated and Catholicism was of the traditional and authoritarian kind. The prevailing attitude to women was expressed in the fact that a wife could not open a bank account without her husband's permission. Parental consent was needed for marriage up to the age of thirty. Children could only be given names listed on an approved, official list. The transformation in recent times has been complete. The Roman Catholic Church has caused considerable anxiety to the Vatican by its progressive attitudes in liturgical matters, ethical attitudes and social involvement. The hold Calvinistic ideas had on society has been vastly reduced, and certainly Amsterdam, in its attitudes to sex, homosexuality, pornography and every possible variation or sexual deviation has become world renowned.

Holland is small. It is, in population terms, extremely dense. Not surprisingly it is tourist minded – on both fronts. The Dutch travel far, perhaps just to get out of a small country. It welcomes tourists in, and is now one of the major tourist centres in the world. Sixty-five per cent of its inhabitants speak English.

The Dutch are by tradition conformist, but by nature individualistic, a combination illustrated aptly in Bosshardt herself. They are courteous and polite, but not effusive. Their ideal, says Huggett, is the golden mean. Proprieties are observed, fun is not lacking, but there is generally a restraint, a controlled politeness not necessarily found in other countries.

Holland is a land of flowers and plants. Window boxes, like those on Bosshardt's sills at the Centre, are typical. It is also the land of the family where primarily and traditionally the man works and the woman rules in the home. It is unusual for mothers with young families to go out to work. The extended family is real and perhaps partly because of this, the phone is almost universal.

'The Dutch live the way they do because they like it and not because they know no other way,' says Huggett. 'They are true conservationists and conservatives (in the non-political sense), retaining all that is worthwhile and appealing from the past.'

'Everything – and everyone – in their proper place' is almost a Dutch maxim. Space is important in a small country. So is order. So the saving of space and harmonious arrangement – of room furniture, window sill ornaments and streets – has been earnestly pursued. The landscape is geometric. And in the streets, at regular hours, the organs play. Huggett sums it up: 'It is difficult and dangerous to generalise about any nation, but there does seem to be an essential duality about the Dutch. They appear to be conformist, a little rigid, and sometimes even disputatious; but, inside, there is always a warm, expansive individual waiting to burst out.' The Dutchman lives 'with his feet firmly planted on the ground, but with his head in the clouds, the practical and pragmatic man and the visionary combined.'

Where then in all this does the Red Light phenomenon fit in? Perhaps most of all it is part of the tolerance the Dutch have demonstrated in their attitudes to both religion and politics, a tolerance surprising in a society with such definite rigidity built into it, yet related in some way to the pragmatism that is so deeply ingrained in the national make-up.

In politics, the Dutch have been democratic to a degree. The right of any political point of view has been stoutly maintained with the inevitable consequence that every government in the Netherlands is a coalition.

Similarly in the religious life of the country there are innumerable sects alongside the mainstream Roman Catholic, Dutch Reformed and Reformed Churches.

The tolerance and pragmatism of the Dutch has led them to be earnest about their own beliefs but equally accepting of the earnestness and authenticity of others' beliefs. They accept the existence of that with which they disagree, however fundamentally, and they totally accept that the right to exist belongs to all points of view.

That then applies to the activity of the Red Light area. If people want pornography, they have a right to it, so it is on sale publicly and in totally respectable bookshops for *all* to buy or simply see – including children. It was this point that I was able to put to Sister Henny as the mother in a family dedicated and devoted to all that is 'good and lovely'.

She did not seem worried and obviously did not feel worried. In fact she found that because her own children were exposed to prostitution as the major activity of their home area and saw daily the kind of publicity for voyeur entertainment of a kind not possible yet in the British society (however far it is felt we have gone downwards in these matters) they were much more able to meet the problems and practicalities of life. That which is open and can be seen loses the attraction of the secret and the fascination of the forbidden.

Bosshardt confirms this point of view from her experience. The children in her area – and there are three thousand of them under eighteen – mature early just because they see wine, sex and prostitution. 'I know how to take care of myself,' said one youngster to the police, 'I know what prostitution is, I have seen it all my life.' Bosshardt claims there are far more problems in the sexual area among protected children who are kept away from anything to do with sex than among the youngsters of her district. They have so much less interest in sex just because it is already a part of their life experience. The only danger is that they may be just too indifferent to it later on. What Bosshardt does claim is that few marriages in her orbit break down, just because of in-built knowledge and thought.

It is a theory that it is not easy to accept. It seems to imply great risk. But coming from such an officer, the testimony of Sister Henny was impressive. It may also bear out the validity of the claim that the way to deal with pornography is not to protest about it, but to ignore it.

That reflects the attitude the Dutch have to the Red Light area. 'Let it be' – for it is a democratic duty to let people have what they want and need, but enclose it tidily in a particular place – for there is a place for everything. The Red Light area is the place for sensuality and for sex in all its forms. There is no need to legalise it formally while to make it illegal is not Dutch practice.

Just let it be – so long as it is kept in its own place.

Live and let live.

It is against that background that it is valuable to look at Bosshardt's view of her responsibility as a Christian and as an Army officer. If the demands of a sex-obsessed society create an ever bigger community of purveyors of pleasure of this particular kind, the Christian faith and The Salvation Army have a duty to minister to that community. While the problems the girls face are as practical as those every member of society faces, there are some that are more specific to the life that is lived. Medical problems would seem to be a particular danger, but in fact medical control and supervision is a normal contribution to the trade. People like Dr. Jan Groothuyse have worked in the Red Light district for over twenty years. Medicine too is essential if the trade is to flourish and tragedy on a huge scale avoided.

But there are the dangers of violence, blackmail, the psychopath, the robber, for by the nature of the work, prostitutes must function alone, however near the pimp, protector or madame. And there are the sad and bitter problems of ageing, the loss of attraction that, pathetically, drives the struggler to poorer premises (for the rooms are hired at considerable rents and paid for by the girls) and lower rates of pay. The profession can be and usually is a lucrative one – and that is why entrants to the profession are numerous – but it can be a struggle and often a lonely one against increasing odds.

How can Bosshardt – or anyone – help? What is there to do not so much by way of prophetic challenge but more by pastoral comfort?

Let Bosshardt herself explain the ministry she is called to give to those who offer their bodies to gain as much of the world as possible, but run the risk of losing their souls.

13

Love For Sale

BOSSHARDT HAS ALWAYS seen her particular ministry in the Red Light area as an expression of the twin responsibilities of the Christian worker – to be an evangelist and to be a social worker. 'Soup, soap and salvation' – it still is as it has always been in the Army. The two disciplines are inseparably bound together for they are parts of ministry to wholeness. And mankind must be ministered to as a whole person.

The ways in which this concept has to be applied to a particular problem have led Colonel Bosshardt to reflect deeply on her specialist work. The detailed knowledge she has of the processes, human and commercial, in 'the trade' have enabled her to make valuable observations on ministry to it.

Prostitution involves not only the girls themselves, but 'a far larger world' behind them – and of course the clients. (It is always strange that in legal attempts to penalise, punish or prevent prostitution, the client comes off best. The girls – in some countries at least – are fined or go to prison. The clients get off altogether). But the 'larger world' also includes the men and women who exploit the girls for financial gain by providing facilities in terms of locations and protection without which 'the trade' is near impossible.

Prostitution is 'the oldest profession' in the world so its present-day existence says nothing particular about our times. It is also universal. Some countries may forbid it, some may tolerate it, but it is there always and so meets some need in the human situation. Its future seems therefore to be assured as a fact of life and living, so it is important to work out both practical treatment and control systems and to evolve ministries that speak and act relevantly to the facts of life.

Bosshardt, like others before her, has found prostitution difficult to define. She quotes the then Chief Justice of Amsterdam (1970) as saying: 'It is extremely difficult to define prostitution, but if you talk about it, everyone knows exactly what you mean.' Bosshardt agrees, but is at least ready to produce the prostitute's own definition which is 'love for sale'. 'She is only fifty per cent correct,' Bosshardt adds. 'She sells – or rather hires – something. Certainly her body. But no one can buy or sell love.'

Prostitution in simplest terms is the offering and giving of sexual relations for gain. The 'love' component is minimal to nil (there may be a degree of affection sometimes). The sexual relations may be heterosexual or homosexual. There may be degrees of perversion involved. Payment, Bosshardt adds, may be in money or kind.

The prostitute is relevantly described as 'common' for she is available generally to all who meet the sum demanded.

As I have commented earlier, the law in the Netherlands does not place prostitution among the offences classified as criminal. There is however an article that states that those third persons who gain their living from the prostitution of others or receive income thus are punishable by law. It is also an offence to persuade immoral acts while on the public highway (that is, loitering). Prostitution is therefore not controlled by law and not forbidden legally. This, as we have noted, represents the tolerant attitude of the country which sees anyone who has reached the age of majority as having a right to the sort of life he or she chooses to live. Others' views on the wrongness, inadequacy or nature of this kind of relationship are irrelevant under such an attitude.

In the area in which Bosshardt lives and works there are estimated to be over three thousand women and girls who are professional prostitutes. These girls work in relays, or shifts. If the average number of clients were eight per day, then something like twenty-four thousand male clients would be received each day by these three thousand girls.

The work of the Goodwill Centre, the Leuwenburgh and the Ruytenburgh is focused particularly on this phenomenal situation.

Bosshardt has classified the prostitutes as (a) those who operate in houses and draw business by posing in windows and standing at doors; and (b) the 'occasional prostitutes' who operate on special days (e.g. market days, etc.) and at the weekends.

'Decent society' looks down on these women but many clients in fact come, usually secretly and surreptitiously, from 'decent society'. The women and girls are therefore used as a service and despised for the service they give – a paradox that produces pain and bitterness in them. The Bosshardt attitude is that there is a ministry to be extended to them in the situation they are in (as we said earlier) and that this ministry is evangelical and social. Salvation Army officers must therefore offer the two-fold, inseparable ministry.

In expounding this theme, Bosshardt, I find, has taken that already quoted story of the woman taken in adultery as her guide-line. Jesus accepted the woman for what she was, in all her humanity, as He accepts us all, placing Himself at her side and not looking down from some lofty pinnacle upon us. He offers us salvation, forgiveness and mercy. The fruit of our personal religious life is seen in the way we follow His example. Therefore, although we do not condone sin, or try to justify the fact of the existence of prostitution, we do try to accept those who have fallen into this way of life and come to their aid in helping them to find a way to something better. We want to bring them the Gospel. If they will accept this, they will find that the broken contact with God will, through Jesus Christ, the Saviour of humanity, be restored.

Bosshardt draws fully on present-day insights into human relations in her approach to the prostitute. 'If we are to help the prostitute from a social point of view, then we must put this work on a level with social work among the aged, industry, the sick and the young.' She goes on:

> We try to help the aged to find adjustment to the realities of becoming older. We try to help the worker find his place in the organisation so that his work is not only satisfying to his employer, but gives him satisfaction too. We try to help those who are ill to adjust to their situation during their incapacity. We try to accompany the young through their difficult years on their way to maturity. Is it not then our task to help the woman or girl who prostitutes herself to adjust to the world of prostitution?
>
> Of course this is not the case! What do we try to do then? We seek to help our fellow human being who is, fundamentally, no different from us except in attitude, to adjust in becoming a woman. It is not natural that any woman should in the course of a night or ten-hour working day receive eight or ten clients for the purpose of sexual intercourse on payment. Living in this way, she has failed to become

adjusted in her womanhood. So with all the modern aids at our disposal as social workers, put to use by skilled and trained helpers, we try to help her, through casework and sometimes in groups, so that she may learn to see herself more clearly and come to want to find a better way of life, in which she can be more fully woman.

To gain insight into herself, to come to herself, to learn to *know* herself – all this happens when Christianity functions properly. Efficient social work functions similarly. Christianity has an extra dimension however. There is a greater power at work. It is a power that can totally change a person and lead to conversion.

So Bosshardt sees her approach, as she repeatedly says, as both evangelical and social. The two strands are inseparable if work is to be cffective. To enable people to help themselves is important, and must be done. But 'real change of character that will bear fruit in due season' depends on 'conversion, the surest means' of change.

Salvation Army officers involved in social work are therefore trying to improve various relationships. The first is the relationship between man and God, the second between man and his neighbour (social relationships) and the third – the relationship of a human being to him or her self. The first involves evangelical work, the second is social work and the third comes about through a combination of both. And referral to psychiatric help must be included in that, if necessary.

The entire work is an expression of our 'love towards God, who gives us the ability to love our fellow-man, regardless of who or what he or she may be. This means the clients of the prostitutes and those who profit from prostitution. All are God's creatures and have a right to renewal of contact with God, through the mercy of His Son, Jesus Christ.'

To seek to fulfil this obligation in word and deed, preaching it and living it daily in the midst of such creatures is the ministry of Alida Bosshardt and all who feel as she does.

That is why she quotes from 'AEM':

> There is no real impoverishment in giving
> And no enrichment if I give to take
> For in such finding, I would lose more deeply
> But, oh, what gain to give for Jesus' sake!

It may be useful to illustrate this from the lives of two more of the girls.

Carla was twenty-one when she came to Amsterdam. Her mother was weak, physically and socially. Her step-father was an easy-going man who concerned himself little with the welfare of his family.

There were four children of the first marriage – Carla was the third of them – and three children of the second marriage. The last three were considerably younger than the earlier four. Mother couldn't and Father wouldn't cope with the family and Carla found herself fed up with it all. There was no home-life, no family life and no feeling of strong attachment to the family. At twenty-one, she left home.

She had a succession of short, unsatisfactory jobs. She became a housemaid, and then a chambermaid in an hotel. She found work in a factory, then drifted on to cafés and hotel night-life.

Carla knew little about human relationships. The nature of her home had left her bereft in this area. She had not acquired the ability to make easy contact with people, far less maintain it. She was in a sense (Bosshardt would put it) 'socially sick'. Inevitably Carla failed at everything she tried. Her relationships were unsatisfactory and her work suffered. The more she, unconsciously, needed and looked for friendship, home-life and love, the further away it seemed to be. Having never known it herself, she could neither give it nor find it.

Inevitably – or nearly so – she found herself in the world of prostitution, for she had followed the path that leads so many in that direction. The combination of parental neglect and poor home-life leading to lack of relationships, the ever-present problem of the need for money and the vague downward drift in search of missing relationships, are forces often present in the making of the prostitute. Carla found in that kind of life a certain amount of distraction, comfort, money and friends.

Her clientele was mainly foreign and as it happened, mainly Chinese. One of these, an older man, attracted her and, while remaining in prostitution, she lived with him and had five children in rapid succession. One of them had a heart defect and died before he was a year old. Carla lived in old Amsterdam with her Chinese friend and their four children in a two-roomed slum, typical of the eight hundred families in that part of the city, Bosshardt's tangled web of cafés, brothels, old people and children, drug-addicts and the displaced.

Carla's younger brother lived with them on the basis that you must help your family, so there were seven people living together in that tiny home. Carla told Bosshardt confidentially that, in fact, only her two boys were the children of her Chinese friend. The girls were by his brother. After the birth of the youngest boy,

Carla married her friend, but for socio-economic reasons, not ethical ones. 'My husband doesn't mind a bit about the girls,' she said, 'so long as they are Chinese; otherwise the neighbours would talk.' Bosshardt asked her if she spoke Chinese. 'Of course not,' she said, 'but it doesn't matter.'

The wedding itself was a major occasion. The idea of marrying in the presence of their children appealed greatly to Carla and her husband-to-be, so the oldest was nine and the youngest three on the great day! Bosshardt is the proud possessor of the photograph of the whole family – Carla, father and the four children.

It took a great deal of intensive social help and support to free Carla from her life of prostitution, but she did get out of it. She attends Salvation Army meetings regularly while the children are involved in young people's activities. Some are Junior Soldiers, some are members of the Tambourine Group. One is in the Brownies. Carla attends the Home League annual camp.

The bringing of both social help and the Christian message into Carla's life has led to a transformation of the whole situation. Collectively and individually, new life and purpose has come into the family and all have gained creatively through the ministry.

Bosshardt had a letter one day from the aunt of a girl called Riet. It said that Riet, her brother's daughter, had been caught up in the prostitution profession for at least two years. Could something be done to help her?

Riet was a nineteen-year-old trainee nurse who was persuaded by a patient who had become a friend to end her nursing training and go with him to Amsterdam. Once there she lived in cheap hotels and poor lodgings and drifted finally through café night-life into prostitution.

One of the great services The Salvation Army has always offered is the Missing Persons Bureau. Through that service, the Goodwill Centre was able to track Riet down in the centre of old Amsterdam where she was living with John. They were not married, but their living came from Riet's work as a prostitute.

For over six months, Bosshardt visited Riet regularly and had long and deep conversations with Riet and her friend. This continued so long and in such a way that it really developed into casework, Bosshardt comments, but it was not as wholly formal and 'structured' as that. Sometimes Bosshardt would meet Riet in a café, when she was on her *War Cry* round. Sometimes it was near one of the stands on the Friday evening district tour. Sometimes it was by appointment in advance, both Riet and John being there on occasion, but at other times Riet alone. Often they came to Bosshardt – or she to them – by night.

It was not easy to talk about religious matters to Riet, but at least some success was achieved in that she began to 'see herself' more clearly. She was able to see that the nature of her attachment to John was a crucial factor in the situation and that it was for his sake and not her own that she was in prostitution. She began to be more in touch with her total life situation and how her place in society was determined by his demands. John put the choice to her in simple terms: 'Stop it if you like, but if you do, I shall find another woman and you will have to go – back to your family or back to nursing.'

In the meantime Bosshardt had made contact with Riet's parents again and as a result knew more of her background.

Riet came from a good middle-class home. She was the second child in the family, but the eldest child, a boy, died young. Because of the sadness this event had brought to the parents, Riet had lacked real attention. Then triplets had been born in the family, and again the parents' attention was concentrated elsewhere, and Riet was – or felt – unloved.

After a year of conversation with Riet, she decided to go home. It was a hard decision to leave John but it had to be made. Having her home again, Riet's parents felt they had to make up for their earlier failures. As a result, Riet felt suffocated and restless. Bosshardt, Riet and the family looked at the new problems together and it was felt it would be best for all and especially for Riet if she worked away from home for a time, so Bosshardt found her work in one of the Army homes for the chronically ill. This she found satisfying. She resumed her nursing training and kept contact with home.

Riet had been brought up in the Protestant Church, but had totally lost contact with it. She went back to church and became a communicant member. Her own testimony, looking back over her experience, was to the value of both the spiritual and social aspects of the work done with her, and she felt that the accepting attitude she associated with the Goodwill Centre had helped her to look at her situation more easily. So her whole life was changed and altered by the ministry carried out by Colonel Bosshardt.

'To serve God we must serve mankind. In serving mankind, we serve God. These two belong together.' So Bosshardt puts it – and lives it.

And Carla and Riet are but two of a very large number of the redeemed of the Red Light area.

14

The Goodwillburgh

MISS BOBELDIJK WAS having a pedicure when I called on her in her home in The Goodwillburgh. Captain Gerben Barkmeyer had told me she was *always* keen to see visitors so that she could show them her lovely little home, so he had chosen her house as the show-house.

Miss Bobeldijk is in her seventies and has lived mostly in the centre of old Amsterdam. As the later part of her life drew nearer, she was loth to leave the place she loved so much, but finding accommodation in her own area was impossible. Like so many others in her position, she feared she must move away, possibly to an outer suburb, possibly out of Amsterdam altogether. Ten or even five years ago, she would have had to do just that. But today she has her lovely little home – thanks to Alida Bosshardt.

We entered the living-room where Miss Bobeldijk sat, her chiropodist busily involved in his professional work. The room was modern, comfortably spacious for someone on her own, and beautifully furnished. As in every Dutch home that I have seen or known, there were plants and flowers everywhere, the ever-present symbols of growth and life. All was neat, clean and very Dutch-orderly! We passed through the living-room to the equally comfortable bedroom, then out again via the splendid bathroom to the hall. You can walk right round the house in a circle (as it were) and be in every part without ever turning back. There were all the other facilities Miss Bobeldijk needed – cupboards, a shower, storage, etc.; and there was an alarm system so that, in any emergency, Miss Bobeldijk could call the warden and summon help.

Miss Bobeldijk lived, in fact, in The Goodwillburgh, the magnificent senior citizens' homes envisaged and brought into being by Colonel Bosshardt. This fine project is an outstanding memorial to its creator and a great benefit to the older and less able people of old Amsterdam.

Let Bosshardt herself tell the story of the genesis of this extraordinary achievement, extraordinary in that it needed a near genius to bring it from conception to completion in terms of (above all) money, but also in terms of official permissions, etc. 'I must say that it was the need of the old people in the centre of Amsterdam that compelled me to think of this project. Like most big cities, Amsterdam has built its new housing estates on the outskirts of the city. But old people who have lived all their lives in the heart of the city, just cannot face up to moving away from their canals and little shops, friends and neighbours to some modern, but unknown district that is out of reach of old, familiar places and is so different from all they have ever known and loved. So we, in the Army, did as we have always done, looked for a solution.'

The Goodwillburgh is the solution, and hundreds now living there 'magnify and bless' Bosshardt for her vision and her concern.

It is again as 'the Salvationist from top to toe' that Bosshardt speaks when she enthuses over the purpose of The Goodwillburgh. 'Our main concern,' she says, 'is – as it should be in The Salvation Army – to bring the Gospel to the people.' Most of the people who live in The Goodwillburgh do not belong to any church and are usually non-Christians. 'So,' says Bosshardt, 'we have ample opportunity to let them feel something of the love and the power of God either by direct spiritual guidance, or by creating a friendly atmosphere in which confidential help can be given when it is needed.' Practical help with all sorts of problems is also given – willingly. Bosshardt goes on, in her (as always) practical way, but a way that also implies a profound sensitivity: 'All these people are coming towards the end of their lives and it is important that they learn to put their trust in the love of God and find their rest in Him.' So everyone in The Goodwillburgh can attend the hall on the premises where social evenings are held and where Sunday worship, evening religious meetings and daily prayers are held. There is no pressure to attend any of these, but many do.

The combination of spiritual depth, associated with the evangelist and common-sense practicality associated with the social worker come out in Bosshardt's explanation of the second purpose of The Goodwillburgh: 'We want the people to look after themselves as long as they can. The houses have been so built (with kitchens, etc.) that people can be free and independent. They bring their own furniture for this reason, but there is the Community Centre and the supervisory arrangements that mean they are in a protected situation and need not feel lonely or left entirely to their own resources.' The Centre provides coffee and chat, courses and hobbies, social meetings, etc. There is a doctor, a social worker and a hairdresser on call. A 'home help' will be provided if necessary and cooked meals can be supplied if the need arises. 'But,' says Bosshardt, 'the main thing is that people can go to their old shops and their old friends and so feel "at home".'

These two statements would seem, by any standards, to provide an adequate philosophy of The Goodwillburgh, but Bosshardt goes further and becomes something of the prophet she is. 'There is another reason for the work. We must go on building a better society for all so that this world may provide a "worthier" life for all. The solution of most of the great problems of our times are beyond our reach, so when we see an opportunity to do anything, however small it is, we must not hesitate but do what we can. It is in this way that most of our social provisions come into being. I consider that, as an Army of the Lord, it is our first duty to recognise needs, find solutions and provide answers. In so doing, we are witnesses for our Lord and Saviour.'

The Goodwillburgh was opened on September 13th, 1975. It cost 8,500,000 guilders. It contains a hundred and two apartments of which eighty-six are for married couples and sixteen are for single people. The building has seven storeys and has two lifts and two fire-escapes.

The Goodwillburgh has frontages on the Anne Frankenstraat, the Niewe Herengeracht and the Rapenburgstraat. The apartments are built round a garden area that has a fountain at its centre while the entry to each apartment is from a balcony facing the gardens. The Community Centre block consists of the large hall, kitchens, a medical room, laundry, hair-dressing salon, reception and waiting rooms, house-keeper's apartments and the social worker's room.

The whole is an absolutely up-to-date complex for older people in Amsterdam and a project of which that city can be proud. But The Goodwillburgh would not be there without the vision, energy, enthusiasm and sheer practical capability of Alida Bosshardt. Everyone in Amsterdam knows that.

When I first saw The Goodwillburgh, it was still 'in the making'. I went with Bosshardt to see the project with which, as I felt, she was crowning all her years of service. We strode through mud and concrete; we stepped over builders' planks; we climbed the, as yet, uncompleted staircase. She talked enthusiastically of what she was doing and laughingly (and triumphantly) of the battles she had had with the authorities to get support and help. There was nothing in her stride that reminded me that she herself was moving towards the 'pensioner' stage. But where would she herself live in the eventide of her life?

Foxes have holes and the birds of the air have nests, but the servants of the Son of Man, for whom home and resting-place can never have been more than rooms 'on the job', can only depend on the organisation to which they belong, giving them a place of some kind somewhere. Was she, I wondered, in fact building her own last nest here beside the people she loved and who loved her? I asked her. She thought this might be so – even if it meant, as it must mean – being virtually on the job for ever! But that too would be Bosshardt for she will never cease to carry the burdens of others this side of eternity. That *is*, for her, the Glory of Life.

In fact, it is to be otherwise. After reflection on that possibility, she told me more recently that there are reasons why she probably should not live there. To these I shall refer in the final chapter. She has instead bought a little house for herself right in the heart of 'her district'.

Perhaps that is the only place for her to be. For, in some profound way, the Red Light area is, as it has been for so long, home.

15

From Café to Temple

DID I DETECT a subtle but significant change in Bosshardt? That was the question in my mind on the last occasion I saw her before the writing of this book was completed. When I first met her two years or so earlier – and on later occasions after that – I felt almost overwhelmed by the sheer weight of her responsibilities, the pressure of her daily commitments and the scope of the work she had created. Empire-builders, whether for material or spiritual ends, run great risks. There is always the danger of the product becoming too big to handle. Bosshardt, I had felt, was near that point. I could not see how any one person, even of so great stature, could continue to cope with the demands of the day and the problems of the night on that scale . . . and it was all still growing. On this, the last occasion, it felt different. Bosshardt was as busy as ever, but there was an objectivity in her of which I had not been so aware previously. For the first time in my experience of her, some 'distance' from the work was developing. With her younger colleagues like Captain Gerben Barkmeyer around her, she was becoming the 'elder statesman' who, though deeply involved, was able to look at the future with a detachment that, though it was almost certainly deliberately adopted, was also being purposely fostered.

There was a time too, earlier, when I had asked myself who, if anyone, was Bosshardt's 'No. 2', for I saw no one in this role. Bosshardt was inspirer, organiser, spiritual director of and to the whole massive operation. The team was there, but organisationally on a much lower rung. Bosshardt stood head and shoulders above it all, spiritual monarch of all she surveyed, even if she was as humble a monarch as ever was. It was different now. There was change taking place around her and at her bidding, and it was clearly change of a considered and constructive kind. What particularly impressed me was the fact that the future organisation of the work had been looked at with such clinical precision. When Bosshardt retired, what she had coped with alone would be shared by three people. First, Captain Barkmeyer would take over as Corps Commander, and be in charge of the 'evangelical' work. Bosshardt's social work role would be placed firmly in a professional social worker's hands, though that team member would not necessarily be a Salvationist – perhaps surprisingly. The third responsibility – that of administration – would involve an expert in that area, i.e. the management and financial care of the Ruytenburgh, the Gastenburgh and the chapel, and so on, would all lie there. So in the *Leger des Heils* (Salvation Army) Goodwill report for 1975 a huge diagram sets out the structure of the empire built by Bosshardt. Under the Headquarters' overall control the '3-manschap and co-ordinator' level would operate (*Korpswerk*, *Sociale Dienst Verblening* and *Ondersteundende Dienst*), directing and managing between them a colossal programme of salvation, soup and the appropriate modern counterparts of soap.

Bosshardt is a charismatic figure and charismatic figures do not die or even fade away. The memories linger on and the successors can find living with such memories something of a trial. Somehow it has now become possible to envisage and work towards a situation in which Bosshardt will cease to be the focal point of the Army's operation in old Amsterdam, but will be present in its life as an honoured, respected and beloved figure.

Can the successors cope with the presence and standing of Bosshardt? I cannot speak of the social work supervisor still, as I write, to come, but in Captain Barkmeyer the Army has found one who will draw on Bosshardt's riches but contribute his own. He and his young wife, of necessity an Army officer, know what they are undertaking and are stimulated by it. They can live creatively with the living memory of Bosshardt, use it for the benefit of the work and make their own contribution in their own way. It is yet another credit to Bosshardt that she has made possible a transition from a personality-centred operation to an organised and 'structured' team approach. The working out of the theory after her retirement will test the ability of all to come to terms with the magic of Bosshardt. I sense it is now possible to do this and this I would have doubted two years ago.

For Bosshardt after June 1978, the diary will be different. But it will be full. After time to re-organise her responsibilities and settle herself in her newly bought house in old Amsterdam, there will be a world tour, and no doubt a long list of engagements and commitments demanded of her by an admiring public. The 'national figure' she has become will be given public platforms that she can use – as she has used every other opportunity – to proclaim the Gospel and its implications. But what a long way this 'top-to-toe Salvationist' has travelled in offering her hand. 'An artist,' writes Charles Jefferson, 'makes himself an artist by painting; a musician makes himself a musician by playing; an athlete makes himself an athlete by running or rowing or wrestling, a merchant makes himself a merchant by buying and selling; and so a Christian makes himself a real Christian by doing Christlike things.' It is in her total self-offering, consistently made over thirty years, that her dedication is displayed and her Lord is shown. That dedication goes deeply into her being. She was saved to save, and knows it.

If any one theme is her favourite, it is *contact*, for contact restores relationship. 'In The Salvation Army as social workers,' she says, 'we seek to improve relationships – the God-man relationship, the man-fellow-man social relationship and the relationship of man to himself. . . . All this must be done because of our love towards God, who gives us the ability to love our fellow-men, whoever or whatever they may be. For me, this means equally the clients of the prostitutes and those who profit from prostitution. All are God's creatures and have a right to renewal of contact with God through the mercy of His Son, Jesus Christ. . . . Conversion is the most sure means of bringing about real change of character.'

I have listened to Bosshardt preach and I have heard her in the quiet of her room in conversation, and all she says is of a piece. She is in no doubt of what she is called to be . . . and do. She lays out her credo constantly. She will convince anyone who hears her. 'Man in his totality is in need, and spirit, mind and body are all involved in that need. Because of a break in contact with God, man has lost his way through life, has lost touch with himself and his fellow men, has become lonely, uncertain, threatened. Man lives in a world which has also rejected God, yet in this world he must find a place and try to make something of his life. The Salvation Army is convinced that man's deepest need is a *spiritual* need . . . God speaks to man in Christ and through His Holy Spirit, and pleads for restored contact.'

Here is my hand – symbol, of a relationship restored . . . has been Bosshardt's perpetual offer in His name.

I have walked from time to time through Bosshardt's district and looked at it all through her eyes.

'How much is that girl in the window?' the passers-by will say. 'God offers *you* His love in Christ whoever you are,' Bosshardt has said.

'Keep away from that man, he is dangerous,' the passer-by would say. Bosshardt would offer that lonely wanderer a cup of coffee.

'That woman's after you, come away,' the passing wife would whisper to her husband. 'She's a deserted woman and is lonely. She needs comfort,' says Bosshardt.

And so (according to Bosshardt) with

the pregnant girl, looking for advice;
the sailor who has a sore head and needs an aspirin;
the 'country cousin' whose money has been stolen and needs a ticket;
the boy hooked on drugs, who wants to be free.

And so they write:

'I come to you because I see no other way out . . .'
'Can you find clothes for myself and my children and for my young baby, and if you can, a cot, a pram, a mattress? I have nothing.'
'I cry as I write this letter. I have so many worries. I am pregnant for a second time. The boy is a sailor and he

never writes to me. I am eight months now and I have nowhere to go. I don't know what to do . . .'

And the result of these thirty years of Goodwill work in the Red Light Area? Bosshardt says:

'Sometimes I can point to success – people who have changed; men, women, children for whom you mean something. What then is the result? You do what you must do; you try hard; you care for all your co-workers. The result? It is God who does the book-keeping.'

The profession of the prostitute can be a particularly dangerous one. There was Blonde Dolly, Jopie, French Henny, Mary, China Anny, Caroline, Tijger, Thin Josje, all with something tragic and terrible in common. They were murdered in the course of their work. How can a girl tell when the client is a psychopath? When a customer will turn into a killer? But 'they were part of us,' says Bosshardt, in taking part in the funeral of one or other of them. They had perhaps been at 'the Major's' last Christmas gathering, singing, laughing, crying, praying.

Praying? But who talks of prayer in the sleazy clubs of the area? What place have the things that are good and lovely and of good report in a sensual, lustful, degrading society?

Enter that sleazy café if you will, or dare. Go quietly, for Bosshardt, the midnight visitor, is there and she *is* praying. Yes, praying as the girls and men, prostitutes and clients, stop the clinking of glasses, the chatter, the raucous laughter.

The immediate area around her is quiet.

Glasses stay still.

Heads are slightly bowed.

It is an unlikely scene.

Bosshardt's voice is quiet, comforting, reassuring.
The silence is near complete.
God is somehow there.
Truly.

'If I descend into hell, Thou art there . . .'

The miracle has happened.
As it does night after night in place after place.
The café, for a brief moment, has under Bosshardt's management, become a temple.

Epilogue

ALIDA BOSSHARDT MIGHT have married. She had the chances to do so. She longed for children but the way she chose to go, as she believed was God's will, was another way.

It has been a way that has cost a lot but profited much. It has been a way that has shown love to God to be loving your neighbour. It is a way that has glorified God, blessed others and still brought the added blessing of self-fulfilment and profound satisfaction.

So Bosshardt, God willing, will go on to help the world to understand what Christian faith is, to show that

The Glory of Life

is

to be a strong hand in the dark
to another in time of need.

'Here is *my* hand.'

Bosshardt stopped to speak to two of 'the girls' as we walked back towards the Goodwill Centre. I heard her say to them that I was (yes, that was a battle I lost!) 'the English preacher'.

The two girls walked towards me, and one held out her hand. I took it in greeting.

The other stepped forward, took both my hands and kissed me lightly on the cheek.

'You won't do the Major any harm, will you?' she asked. 'We love her.'

I hope I have not done Bosshardt harm.

It would be the last thing I should want to do to one who has always gone about 'doing good'.

She has done this, not to her own, but to God's glory.

That *is* the Glory of Life.

OTHER SALVATION ARMY TITLES FROM HODDER & STOUGHTON

A Thoroughly Modern Martha

Mary Endersbee

The Life of Brigadier Martha Field

'Sometimes,' says Brigadier Martha Field, 'I walk the streets and my feet are aching and my heart too, for that matter, and I look to the sky and say, "Oh, boy, what you've let me in for, General!" '

The name Martha Field is mentioned with affection and respect by policemen, ambulance drivers, doctors, nurses, social workers and, of course, her own officer colleagues in The Salvation Army. Following in the steps of William Booth she has given her life to people in need. Her ministry has been in the cities where, as this book reveals, there is little room for complacency.

'Compelling, because it is the story of strong goodness defeating evil at its hardest points.' – ***Church of England Newspaper.***

Hugh Redwood: With God in Fleet Street

William Clark

The story of Hugh Redwood, author of 'God in the Slums'

Hugh Redwood's story of The Salvation Army became an international bestseller. Now an officer of The Salvation Army has written this biography of the Fleet Street journalist whose life was dramatically changed by an unexpected encounter.

Hugh Redwood arrived at Westminster in the aftermath of floods, and found himself assisting Salvation Army Officers caring for flood victims. Thus began a relationship with the happiest consequences: Redwood used his talents as speaker and writer to broadcast the ministry of The Salvation Army with *God in the Slums* and other titles, attracting worldwide attention. Until his death he was an untiring witness in Fleet Street, where he worked for nearly fifty years.

'A most moving account of a hard-bitten professional's pilgrimage to God and the influence The Salvation Army played in his life.' – *Church of Ireland Gazette*

The Midnight Patrol

Phyllis Thompson

The story of Brigadier Mary Scott, a woman prepared to look sin in the face – see it for the horrible thing it is – and in the name of Christ to do something about it.

In the early 1950s the British Government asked The Salvation Army to help rescue girls in danger of being drawn into London's blatant prostitution racket. It was decided to recommence the 'Midnight Patrol', discontinued due to the war, dedicated to looking nightly for young girls alone and adrift in London's streets or arriving at main line stations. The right person had to be found, someone with the right appearance, the right approach, the quick-wittedness and compassion. Mary Scott was the answer.

'The kind of woman who is the glory and strength of The Salvation Army.' – *Church Times*

Missing!

Richard Williams

Each year thousands of people disappear from their homes, often never to be heard of again. Even in the most highly organised countries it is easy for a person to vanish without trace.

With skill, shrewdness and compassion The Salvation Army maintains a world-wide service for the families of missing people. Each Salvationist is conscious that at all times hundreds of distressed, despairing people are pinning their hopes on him and his fellow-workers.

Lieut.-Colonel Williams writes from a wealth of personal experience, with a warm humanity and lively sense of the individual's essential worth.